BACK LANE WINERIES *of* SONOMA

BACK LANE WINERIES

OF

SONOMA

Second Edition

TILAR MAZZEO
PHOTOGRAPHY BY PAUL HAWLEY

TEN SPEED PRESS
Berkeley

Previous edition originally published in the United
States by The Little Bookroom, New York, in 2009.

All photographs by Paul Hawley with the exception
of the following:
Page 86: Garden Creek Ranch Vineyard Winery
Page 101: Hawley Winery
Page 145: Siduri Wines
Page 147: Pellegrini Family Vineyards
Page 153: Tara Bella Winery & Vineyards
Page 164: Thomas George Estates
Page 218–219: La Rue Wines
Page 221: Dustan Wine

Library of Congress Cataloging-in-Publication Data
Mazzeo, Tilar J.
  The back lane wineries of Sonoma / Tilar J.
Mazzeo ; photographs by Paul Hawley. – Second
edition.
    pages cm
  Includes index.
1. Wine tourism—California—Sonoma County.
2. Wine tasting—California—Sonoma County.
3. Wineries—California—Sonoma County—
Guidebooks. 4. Sonoma County (Calif.)—
Guidebooks. I. Title.
  TP548.5.T68M39 2014
  663'.20979418—dc23
                                    2013032084

Trade Paperback ISBN: 978-1-60774-592-1
eBook ISBN: 978-1-60774-593-8

Printed in China

Design by Katy Brown
Cartography by Moon Street Cartography,
Durango, Colorado

10 9 8 7 6 5 4 3 2 1

Second edition

Contents

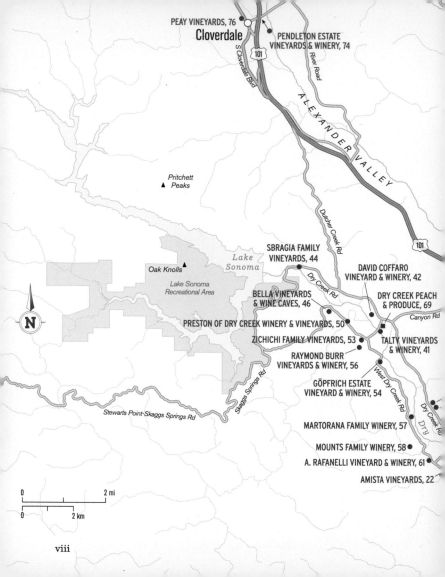

PEAY VINEYARDS, 76
Cloverdale
PENDLETON ESTATE
VINEYARDS & WINERY, 74

S Cloverdale Blvd

River Road

101

A L E X A N D E R   V A L L E Y

▲ Pritchett
Peaks

Dutcher Creek Rd

101

Lake
Sonoma

SBRAGIA FAMILY
VINEYARDS, 44

Oak Knolls ▲

DAVID COFFARO
VINEYARD & WINERY, 42

Lake Sonoma
Recreational Area

Dry Creek Rd

BELLA VINEYARDS
& WINE CAVES, 46

DRY CREEK PEACH
& PRODUCE, 69

Canyon Rd

N

PRESTON OF DRY CREEK WINERY & VINEYARDS, 50

ZICHICHI FAMILY VINEYARDS, 53

TALTY VINEYARDS
& WINERY, 41

RAYMOND BURR
VINEYARDS & WINERY, 56

West Dry Creek Rd

Skaggs Springs Rd

GÖPFRICH ESTATE
VINEYARD & WINERY, 54

Dry Creek Rd

Stewarts Point-Skaggs Springs Rd

MARTORANA FAMILY WINERY, 57

D R Y

MOUNTS FAMILY WINERY, 58

A. RAFANELLI VINEYARD & WINERY, 61

AMISTA VINEYARDS, 22

0   2 mi

0   2 km

viii

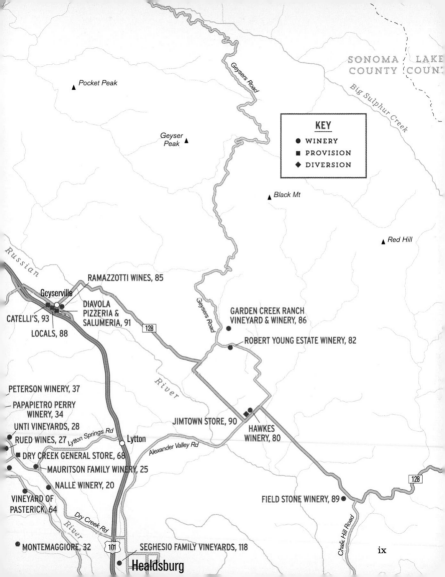

KEY

- ● WINERY
- ■ PROVISION
- ◆ DIVERSION

SONOMA COUNTY / LAKE COUNTY

Pocket Peak ▲

Geyser Peak ▲

Black Mt ▲

Red Hill ▲

Geysers Road

Big Sulphur Creek

Russian River

RAMAZZOTTI WINES, 85

Geyserville

DIAVOLA PIZZERIA & SALUMERIA, 91

CATELLI'S, 93

LOCALS, 88

128

GARDEN CREEK RANCH VINEYARD & WINERY, 86

ROBERT YOUNG ESTATE WINERY, 82

Geysers Road

River

PETERSON WINERY, 37

PAPAPIETRO PERRY WINERY, 34

UNTI VINEYARDS, 28

RUED WINES, 27

Lytton Springs Rd

Lytton

JIMTOWN STORE, 90

HAWKES WINERY, 80

Alexander Valley Rd

DRY CREEK GENERAL STORE, 68

MAURITSON FAMILY WINERY, 25

NALLE WINERY, 20

128

VINEYARD OF PASTERICK, 64

FIELD STONE WINERY, 89

Dry Creek Rd

River

Chalk Hill Road

MONTEMAGGIORE, 32

101

SEGHESIO FAMILY VINEYARDS, 118

Healdsburg

ix

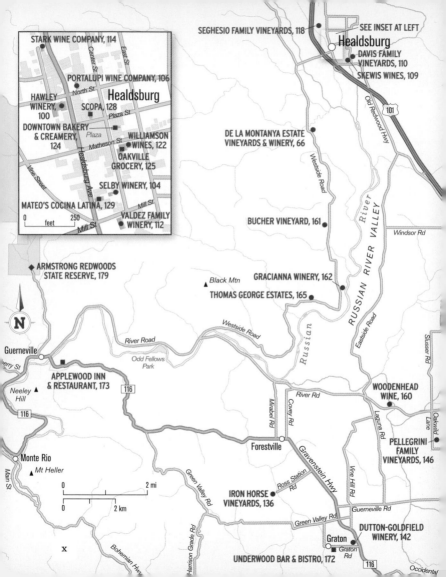

SEGHESIO FAMILY VINEYARDS, 118

SEE INSET AT LEFT

Healdsburg

DAVIS FAMILY VINEYARDS, 110

SKEWIS WINES, 109

101

DE LA MONTANYA ESTATE VINEYARDS & WINERY, 66

Westside Road

RUSSIAN RIVER VALLEY

Windsor Rd

BUCHER VINEYARD, 161

River

Eastside Road

Slusser Rd

ARMSTRONG REDWOODS STATE RESERVE, 179

Black Mtn

GRACIANNA WINERY, 162

THOMAS GEORGE ESTATES, 165

N

Westside Road

Russian

Guerneville

Cherry St

River Road

Odd Fellows Park

116

APPLEWOOD INN & RESTAURANT, 173

Neeley Hill

116

Monte Rio

Mt Heller

Mirabel Rd

Covey Rd

River Rd

WOODENHEAD WINE, 160

Laguna Rd

Vine Hill Rd

Oakwild Lane

PELLEGRINI FAMILY VINEYARDS, 146

Forestville

Gravenstein Hwy

0   2 mi

0   2 km

Green Valley Rd

Ross Station Rd

IRON HORSE VINEYARDS, 136

Guerneville Rd

Main St

X

Bohemian Hwy

Harrison Grade Rd

Green Valley Rd

Graton

Graton Rd

DUTTON-GOLDFIELD WINERY, 142

UNDERWOOD BAR & BISTRO, 172

116

Occidental

Inset (Healdsburg)

STARK WINE COMPANY, 114

Center St

East St

PORTALUPI WINE COMPANY, 106

North St

Healdsburg

HAWLEY WINERY, 100

SCOPA, 128

Plaza St

DOWNTOWN BAKERY & CREAMERY, 124

Plaza

WILLIAMSON WINES, 122

Matheson St

Healdsburg Ave

OAKVILLE GROCERY, 125

Vine Street

SELBY WINERY, 104

MATEO'S COCINA LATINA, 129

Mill St

VALDEZ FAMILY WINERY, 112

0   feet   250

Mill St

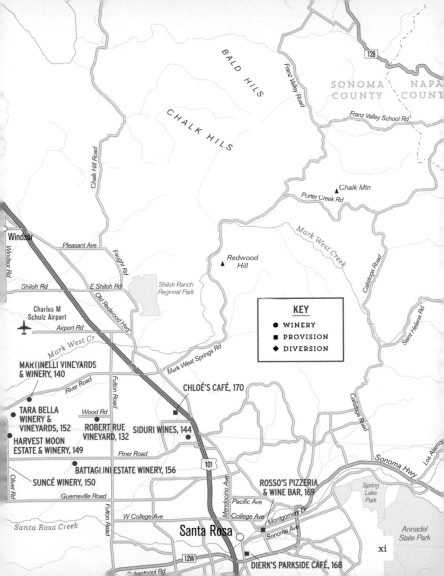

BALD HILLS

CHALK HILLS

SONOMA COUNTY

NAPA COUNTY

128

Franz Valley Road

Franz Valley School Rd

Chalk Hill Road

Chalk Mtn

Porter Creek Rd

Mark West Creek

Windsor

Pleasant Ave

Faught Rd

Redwood Hill

Calistoga Road

Saint Helena Rd

Windsor Rd

Shiloh Rd

E Shiloh Rd

Old Redwood Hwy

Shiloh Ranch Regional Park

Charles M Schulz Airport

Airport Rd

Mark West Cr

Mark West Springs Rd

KEY

● WINERY
■ PROVISION
◆ DIVERSION

MARTINELLI VINEYARDS & WINERY, 140

River Road

Fulton Road

CHLOÉ'S CAFÉ, 170

TARA BELLA WINERY & VINEYARDS, 152

Wood Rd

ROBERT RUE VINEYARD, 132

SIDURI WINES, 144

HARVEST MOON ESTATE & WINERY, 149

Piner Road

101

BATTAGLINI ESTATE WINERY, 156

SUNCÉ WINERY, 150

Oliver Rd

Guerneville Road

Mendocino Ave

ROSSO'S PIZZERIA & WINE BAR, 169

Sonoma Hwy

Los Alamos

Spring Lake Park

Calistoga Road

Pacific Ave

W College Ave

College Ave

Montgomery Dr

Fulton Road

Santa Rosa

Sonoma Ave

Santa Rosa Creek

12W

DIERK'S PARKSIDE CAFÉ, 168

Annadel State Park

12W
Santa Rosa

West Ave

101

Stony Point Road

Santa Rosa Avenue

Bennett Valley Rd

BENNETT VALLEY

Annadel State Park

12

Kenwood

Petaluma Hill Rd

Grange Rd

Bennett Valley Rd

Warm Springs Rd

Sonoma

Golf Course Dr

SONOMA MOUNTAINS

Sonoma Mtn

Jack London State Park

101

116

N

Rohnert Park

Petaluma Hill Road

Cotati

Old Redwood Hwy

Stony Point Road

Pepper Road

0   2 mi

0   2 km

Redwood Hwy

Corona Rd

Old Adobe Road

Sonoma Mountain Pkwy

Washington St

Petaluma Airport

Old Adobe Rd

McDowell Blvd

101

Bodega Ave

Frates Rd

Petaluma

xii

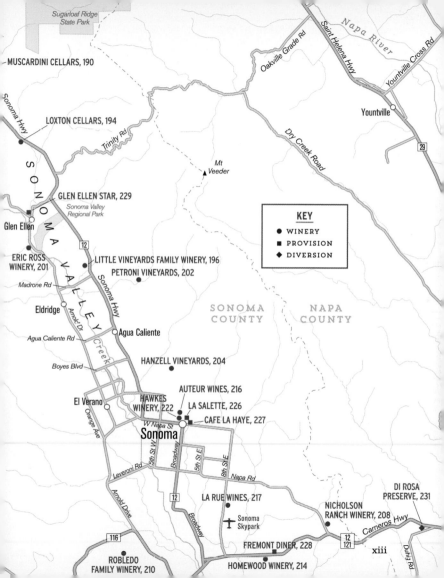

Sugarloaf Ridge
State Park

MUSCARDINI CELLARS, 190

Napa River

LOXTON CELLARS, 194

Oakville Grade Rd

Saint Helena Hwy

Yountville Cross Rd

Sonoma Hwy

Trinity Rd

Yountville

Dry Creek Road

29

*Mt
Veeder*

GLEN ELLEN STAR, 229

Sonoma Valley
Regional Park

Glen Ellen

12

SONOMA VALLEY

ERIC ROSS
WINERY, 201

LITTLE VINEYARDS FAMILY WINERY, 196

PETRONI VINEYARDS, 202

Madrone Rd

Sonoma Hwy

Eldridge

Arnold Dr

SONOMA
COUNTY

NAPA
COUNTY

Agua Caliente Rd

Agua Caliente

Boyes Blvd

HANZELL VINEYARDS, 204

Sonoma Creek

El Verano

AUTEUR WINES, 216

HAWKES
WINERY, 222

LA SALETTE, 226

Orange Ave

CAFE LA HAYE, 227

W Napa St
Sonoma

5th St W

Broadway

5th St E

8th St E

Leveroni Rd

Napa Rd

12

DI ROSA
PRESERVE, 231

Arnold Drive

LA RUE WINES, 217

Sonoma
Skypark

NICHOLSON
RANCH WINERY, 208

Carneros Hwy

116

Broadway

FREMONT DINER, 228

12
121

Duhig Rd

xiii

ROBLEDO
FAMILY WINERY, 210

HOMEWOOD WINERY, 214

KEY

● WINERY
■ PROVISION
◆ DIVERSION

THE WINES IN SONOMA COUNTY are world-class, and each year more than 7.5 million tourists visit what locals call simply "the North Bay"—the rural and still magical wine country less than an hour north of San Francisco. And everyone knows, of course, that wine tasting is a serious business. Swirl, sniff, taste. There is nothing wrong with classiness and expertise and the love of a fine wine. This is the stuff *la dolce vita* is made of.

But the wine country is also, increasingly, big business. Many tasting rooms are slick retail operations run by corporate managers living somewhere a long way from Sonoma, offering wines that you can buy just as readily (and often less expensively) on the shelves of your local grocery store. Often, these are beautiful places, and I am not recommending that you pass them by entirely. A part of the California wine tasting experience is sitting on marbled Italianate terraces overlooking acres of perfectly pruned vineyards, basking in the warm sun and the intense loveliness of it all.

But you don't need a guidebook to see this part of the North Bay wine country. Highway 101 is plastered with billboards, and you would be hard-pressed to miss the big-name tasting rooms clustered around the central plazas of quaint towns like Sonoma, Healdsburg, or Glen Ellen (all worth a leisurely visit).

Just as exciting and often far more difficult to spot, however, are the small, back lane wineries of Sonoma, places that the critics, industry professionals, and locals revere but few visitors ever see. These are wineries run by the same people who grow the grapes and make the wines, and they are geared toward curious travelers looking to discover what it is about Sonoma County that makes everyone who lives here swear it is paradise.

This is a guide to those back lane wineries of Sonoma County. Places where you can find excellent handcrafted wines made by on-site proprietors, often with only a local or regional distribution and a limited case production. The vast majority of the wineries included in this book make fewer than ten thousand cases of wine a year, and the smallest produce only a hundred or two. The very largest make fewer than thirty-five thousand cases, and, in a county where some of the big commercial operations churn out five million cases of wine a year, this is still a small operation. Off the beaten path there are few marbled terraces or stucco palaces, but often these wineries are in the midst of striking beauty—overlooking a hundred acres of a wildlife preserve, on the edge of an ancient redwood forest, or tucked along a rural side road in the middle of open fields, where the proprietors are happy to watch you settle down for a picnic with a bottle or two of wine.

Best of all, in my mind, these are places where wine tasting gets down to earth. These are places where no one needs to show off how developed his or her palate is and where the winemakers welcome questions, from beginners and experts alike. Often, you will also find that these are the wineries where sustainable and organic viticulture is being pioneered. And, above all, these are wines that are likely to be a new experience, with names that you won't find in big retail outlets back home. Amid the back lane wineries of Sonoma, you can still make secret discoveries.

How to Use This Book

THE SONOMA COUNTY WINE REGION is made up of more than a dozen appellations and subappellations, some of them quite small, each with a particular microclimate and with particular grape varietals that thrive in the region. Most of the wineries in the area can be reached by traveling along one of two local highways, Highway 101, which runs in the north-south direction, and Highway 12, which intersects with Highway 101 near Santa Rosa and runs roughly in the east-west direction.

Sonoma County covers a relatively large area, and, because it can easily take more than an hour of steady driving to get across the region, the best way to plan a day of wine tasting is to focus on just one or two appellations, taking time for a leisurely gourmet lunch and some sightseeing along the way. This guide is arranged by region, and at the end of each section are suggestions for nearby restaurants or local attractions that you can work into an itinerary spontaneously.

This book divides the county into five primary areas that, working south along Highway 101, include:

DRY CREEK VALLEY (Chapter 1; shown on maps on pages viii–ix), west of Highway 101 at Healdsburg, focuses on Zinfandel, Cabernet, and Sauvignon Blanc and includes the Dry Creek Valley and Rockpile American Viticultural Areas (AVAs).

ALEXANDER VALLEY (Chapter 2; shown on maps on pages viii–ix), northeast of Highway 101 at Healdsburg, focuses on Cabernet and Chardonnay and includes the Alexander Valley and Knight's Valley AVAs.

HEALDSBURG (Chapter 3; shown on maps on pages x–xi), along Highway 101, is a charming little boutique town where many small producers have tasting rooms.

RUSSIAN RIVER VALLEY (Chapter 4 shown on maps on pages x–xi), west of Highway 101 at Windsor, focuses on Chardonnay and Pinot Noir and includes the Russian River Valley, Sonoma Coast, Green Valley, and Chalk Hill AVAs.

SONOMA VALLEY (Chapter 5; shown on maps on pages xii–xiii), east of Highway 101 at Santa Rosa, along Highway 12, and south of the town of Sonoma along Highway 121, focuses on Cabernet Sauvignon, Merlot, Zinfandel, Pinot Noir, and Chardonnay, as well as sparkling wines in the traditional "champagne" style and includes the historic town of Sonoma and the surrounding Sonoma Valley, Sonoma Mountain, Bennett Valley, and Los Carneros AVAs.

All the wineries listed in this book are open to visitors in some fashion or another, and wine tasting hours throughout the county are generally from 10 a.m. to 4:30 p.m. daily, although some wineries have longer or shorter hours, and it is always a good idea to call ahead to confirm opening times, especially early in the week (Monday and Tuesday particularly). Groups larger than six people should always call ahead to make sure the winemakers can accommodate you.

Many of the best small wineries are open by appointment only, and you should not feel in the least bit shy about making the call. It just means that the winemaker wants to be sure he or she knows to staff the tasting room that afternoon, and it is usually a sign that the person behind the bar will be the same person who goes out pruning the vines other days of the week. Often, these winemaker tours are exceptional educational experiences and a rare opportunity to get an inside perspective on the craft of wine-making. Generally, it's a good idea to call a week in advance of your trip to set up appointments (and at a few places there are long waiting lists, which are noted in the particular entries). But should you find yourself in the wine country unexpectedly, there's absolutely no harm in making a spur-of-the-moment call. Often, the winemakers are able to welcome even last-minute visitors.

When you are planning your trip, keep in mind that weekends are the busiest time for wine tasting, especially at the commercial wineries and in summer, where you will often have to jostle for a place at the tasting bar. A busy Saturday is the perfect time to head off the beaten path and visit some of the back lane wineries. Locals prefer to go wine tasting on Thursday and Friday mornings, when most places are open and gearing up for the weekend. And if you are hoping to visit in September, plan with particular care. The harvest—known in Sonoma County as "the crush"—takes place around then, and the tasting room hours can be limited. But there are often opportunities to participate in other special events and harvest suppers during what can be one of the most festive times of the winemaking year.

And what will all this cost? Many tasting rooms (and nearly all the commercial ones) charge modest tasting fees, typically ranging from $5 to $15 for a "flight" of wines—a small taste of several different wines. It generally costs a bit more to taste premium "reserve" wines ($20 and up is common), and the best of those experiences are sit-down private appointments with a winemaker that can last an hour or more. For wine-education or food-and-wine pairing experiences, $40 and up is common—but generally worth it if you want a real behind-the-scenes tour or if you only want to visit one or two wineries daily. If you want to visit several wineries, no one will mind in the least if you ask to share a flight with your tasting companions, and in many cases the cost of your tasting fees will be waived if you buy even a single bottle of wine.

In some places, especially in the smaller back-road wineries, there will be no charge for tasting and no charge even for the winemaker tours, and there is never any obligation to buy wine when out tasting. But winemaking is an expensive business, and for many of these small proprietors this is a labor of love. Buying someone's wine after you've enjoyed it is the best compliment, and my own rule of thumb for wine tasting etiquette is that, if there is no charge for the tasting, the polite thing to do is buy a couple of bottles. When there is a charge for the tasting, I buy only the wines I know I will enjoy. But because tasting fees are so often waived with a purchase, it never makes any sense to me not to buy a bottle at each winery.

If you don't have room to take it home, many of the best local restaurants here in wine country charge only a modest corkage fee for opening your own special bottle tableside. In Sonoma County, gourmet food is one of the great community passions. Almost every day of the week in the summer there are open-air farmers' markets in the local town squares, where families gather to

listen to jazz on cool evenings and dine al fresco out of their canvas shopping bags. The grocery stores offer a dizzying array of homemade cheese and artisan breads, and the local park rangers offer classes in mushroom hunting each autumn. But when it comes to food, the North Bay wine country is most famous for its restaurants—and rightly so. The restaurant recommendations in this guide highlight places where you are welcome to enjoy your most recent discovery—places that also have excellent local wine lists, where perhaps new discoveries await. And in a corner of the world blessed with an abundance of riches, these are also the kind of restaurants where you can while away a long afternoon when the pressures of wine tasting become overwhelming or where you can settle in for a lovely dinner worth celebrating.

Wine Tasting Essentials

EVEN SOPHISTICATED WINE AFICIONADOS sometimes find themselves wondering what the "right" way to taste wine is, and, as you anticipate sitting down face-to-face with a winemaker, it's easy to start worrying about whether you'll pass the test. But there's no need. In the wine country, the friendliest welcome of all is reserved for passionate amateurs. And you're not the only one who gets the giggles when that gentleman at the far end of the tasting bar starts throwing around wildly improbable adjectives. The winemakers do, too.

If you want to refresh yourself on the basics before throwing yourself into your wine tasting adventures, it's easily done. For starters, hold the wine glass by the stem. Cupping it in your hands and leaving greasy fingerprints not only looks decidedly unglamorous, but this will also warm the wine, changing its aromas. And the experts will tell you that "tasting" wine is largely about aroma. We can experience only six different tastes, and nature's way around the limited range of our taste buds is to marry those perceptions to the thousand or more different smells that we can detect, creating seemingly endless delights for the gourmet. This is the whole point of swirling and sniffing your wine.

When you are handed a glass—and your tasting typically will progress from the lightest wine to the most intense wine in the flight—begin by gently tilting it to look at the clarity and colors if you like. Unless you're an expert, the conclusion you'll probably reach is that it looks delicious. But a trained eye will be looking to assess alcohol content, barrel aging, and structural components. Then, give the glass a swirl. Many of us accomplish this most gracefully by keeping the glass on the table and making a few quick circles, but if you're the daring sort, there's always the riskier midair execution to perfect as the afternoon wears on. The point is that the movement begins to open the bouquet of the wine. You are supposed to start with a gentle sniff with your nose above the glass, then move on to a deeper sniff with your nose right down there in the stemware. As a wine drinker and not a contest judge, what you're looking for is a sensory experience that will help you pick out the different aromas that shape how this wine is going to taste for you.

The next step—finally—is to take a sip of wine. Remember that the taste buds are in your mouth and not down your gullet. So roll the wine around in your mouth for a few moments, making sure it reaches the different parts of your tongue, where the distinct tastes and textures are experienced. Before you swallow, you can also try pulling a little air over your teeth and breathing in through your nose to aspirate the wine and intensify the experience of the aroma.

There is also a technique where you can attempt to slurp the wine silently and draw the vapors into your sinuses, usually affected by placing your tongue on the outside of the glass as you drink and inhaling simultaneously. If you do it right, the result is what the experts call retro-olfaction—a concentrated explosion of aroma that takes the information your brain needs to process smell more directly to your neurological receptors. But if you do it wrong, you'll end up sputtering wine rather dramatically. It might be wise to practice at home first. Or if you find yourself wine tasting without an audience, ask one of the winemakers you'll meet out in the far corners of Sonoma County to show you how it's done.

In the course of your tasting adventures, you may also see some fellow tasters spit the wine out without swallowing. That's perfectly acceptable, and it's the reason tasting rooms have those dump buckets on the counter. All those little sips of wine add up quickly, after all. And remember: no matter how much fun you are having, drinking from the dump bucket happens only in the movies.

Shipping Wines Home

FOR MANY VISITORS to the wine country of Sonoma County, the trouble is finding ways to get all these wonderful wines home. When you have been touring the back lane wineries, discovering small-production, handcrafted wines that won't be available at home, the question takes on a particular urgency. Most of the wineries in this book distribute their wines only through their tasting room sales, and this is part of what makes discovering them so satisfying.

Depending on where you live, there are several excellent options for getting your purchases back to your home cellar. Many wineries will ship your purchases home to you directly, provided your state allows this. The costs are generally prohibitive for a single bottle of wine, but for several it is quite reasonable. For purchases of a case of more, ask whether there is flexibility in their wine club program. The club discounts are often significant, and generally your only commitment is agreeing to purchase a case of wine over the course of the year. Often, the wineries want to ship the wines to you quarterly, but, when we wanted to get a few cases to our summer place in New England, I never had any trouble persuading the local winemakers to send me the entire annual allotment at once, at a significant savings in the shipping.

Or you can send it as checked luggage. I have done it for years and only rarely has a bottle broken en route. A sturdy cardboard box, marked fragile, can get an entire case of wine across the country with minimal hassle, provided you understand the airline policies and your state sales-tax regulations. And here's my favorite wine country secret: you can fly on several commercial airlines directly in and out of the airport in Santa Rosa. In addition to saving the hour-and-a-half drive from Bay Area airports and starting your wine country weekend that much sooner, Horizon Air (an Alaska Airlines partner) doesn't currently charge you for the first case of wine shipped home as checked luggage (details at sonomacountyairport.org). Most wineries will happily give you a regular packing box, and some of the wineries have started selling extra-sturdy boxes specifically designed for sending wines this way. You can also purchase a wine-lover's suitcase from catalog suppliers before your trip and rest easy, knowing that your only worry is finding favorite wines to fill it up.

For those extra-special, high-end purchases destined for the cellar of the serious collector, there are always third-party shippers who specialize in sending wines anywhere you need them to go. At the end of the guide (page 232), I list my top picks, or you can ask at any premium winery for the staff recommendations.

Even if you take nothing home with you as a souvenir for your cellar, the back lane wineries of Sonoma are an experience few visitors ever forget. Off the beaten path and along the back roads, amid oak trees and mustard blooms, the experience of wine tasting is immediate and personal. May your journey and discoveries be as individual as your palate, and welcome to the heart of Sonoma County.

Sauvignon Blanc

DRY CREEK VALLEY
SONOMA COUNTY

CHAPTER 1

DRY CREEK VALLEY

WINERIES

PROVISIONS

Maps on pages viii–ix

THIS LITTLE SLIVER OF A VALLEY in northern Sonoma County is home to some of California's finest Zinfandels, which thrive in the dry, hot summers in this part of the wine country. The appellation is also known for its excellent Cabernet Sauvignon, Merlot, and—increasingly—its less familiar Italian and southern French varietals.

When tasting in the appellation, it is easy to confuse Dry Creek Road with West Dry Creek Road. The two run roughly parallel to each other in a north-south direction through the valley, and both roads are home to some of the region's best back lane discoveries. You could do a full day of tasting on either route. But, for dedicated wine enthusiasts, my favorite circuit begins by taking the Dry Creek exit from Highway 101 and tasting your way north along Dry Creek Road as far as Yoakim Bridge Road, which heads west and intersects with West Dry Creek Road. If you then taste your way south on West Dry Creek Road, you can either call it quits and head back to Highway 101 via Lambert Bridge Road or continue south until West Side Road. You can pick up free road maps at almost any tasting room or hotel in the wine country.

THE SELF-PROCLAIMED motto of the Nalle family is *vinum sapientiam tibi dat*. For anyone whose Latin is a bit on the rusty side that roughly translates to "wine makes you smart." And it's those handy opposable thumbs—so perfect for holding wine glasses—that separate us from the primordial pollywogs. It's all just part of nature's "zintelligent" design. That's what one of the witty T-shirts displayed on coat hangers in the winery's tasting room announces.

This laid-back fun-loving approach—combined with a single-minded passion for making great wines—is what the Nalle family winery, run by Lee and Doug Nalle and their son, Andrew, is all about. There's nothing stuffy or pretentious here about wine or winemaking. They have been quietly making acclaimed small-lot wines since the early 1980s, and their tasting room does double duty as a storage facility. In fact, it is one of Sonoma County's few aboveground caves—the building is covered with sod and planted with the fragrant rosemary that grows so easily in the North Bay's Mediterranean climate. The purpose of this unique structure, however, is all about winemaking: the soil creates an ideal climate for aging wines, naturally regulating both the temperature and the humidity in a fashion that is at once traditional and ecologically sustainable.

Despite the ironic irreverence of the wine marketing at Nalle, the wines ($40 to $45) are nothing but serious. Their Zinfandel, a Dry Creek classic, is made from the field blend of eighty-seven-year-old vines growing right out in front of the tasting room. Behind the winery is a Cabernet Sauvignon and Merlot vineyard that is now being used for their Henderlong Ranch Bordeaux blend. With grapes from the Hopkins Ranch vineyard in the Russian River Valley, they also craft a Chardonnay and an excellent Burgundy-style Pinot Noir.

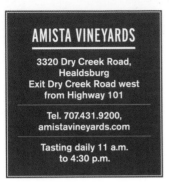

MICHAEL AND VICKY FARROW started dreaming of a life in the Dry Creek wine country back when they were young and first dating. On one romantic trip to the area, they fell in love with Sonoma County. But life had other plans for the couple. Mike's PhD in chemistry led him to the computer industry, and Vicky had a high-flying career as a corporate executive. But even then they had planted the backyard of their suburban home in the Santa Clara Valley with 150 Cabernet Sauvignon vines, and Mike started making garage wines for their family and friends.

Mike and Vicky will tell you that friends have always been at the heart of this enterprise. The name Amista—which roughly translates as "making friends"—is a nod to all the people along the way who encouraged them to pursue this shared passion. In 1999, they finally bought twenty-eight acres of ranch land on the eastern banks of the Dry Creek, and in 2003—at the age when most folks are beginning to dream of retirement—they released their first commercial vintage. Today, their rustic barn-style tasting room lies down the end of a long gravel lane set up against the foothills, and, with the help of their consulting winemaker Ashley Herzberg, the couple produces around twenty-five hundred cases a year of Dry Creek classics: estate Chardonnay, Syrah, and rosé of Syrah, plus Zinfandel and Cabernet, all in the $20 to $45 range. They are the only winery in the Dry Creek to produce estate-grown sparkling wines made in the traditional *méthode champagneoise*.

YOU MIGHT FIND yourself thinking that Clay Mauritson—the tour de force behind the Mauritson Family Winery—is part of a new generation of winemakers in Sonoma County. And certainly there is nothing old-fashioned or stuffy about the elegant and gleaming tasting rooms where he'll welcome you to sample some wines.

But the Mauritson family is anything but a newcomer in this valley, and Clay is the sixth generation to raise grapes on the estate properties. In fact, just a bit farther north, in the newly designated (and aptly named) Rockpile appellation, his pioneering Swedish ancestors planted the first vines in the area back in the 1880s. Thanks to the Warm Springs Dam and the Army Corps of Engineers, much of that sprawling ranch land today lies at the bottom of Lake Sonoma, but Clay and his wife, Carrie, continue to make distinctive Zinfandel, Cabernet Sauvignon, Syrah, Malbec, and Petite Sirah wines from fruit grown in the high-elevation vineyards that survived. If you've never tried a wine from the Rockpile appellation, you're in for a treat. It's a sparse and rugged landscape, where the vines suffer and the fruit is beautifully intense.

There are also estate wines made from fruit grown on family properties in the Dry Creek and Alexander Valley appellations, including a small-lot Chardonnay, a rosé, and a Sauvignon Blanc. Most wines range from $20 to $50.

MAURITSON FAMILY WINERY

2859 Dry Creek Road, Healdsburg
Exit Dry Creek Road west from Highway 101, at the Lytton Springs Road intersection

Tel. 707.431.0804, mauritsonwines.com

Tasting daily 10 a.m. to 5 p.m.; winemaker and vineyard tours by appointment only

THE RUED WINES tasting room is one of the new additions to the dozen or more wineries that have opened along Dry Creek Road, but Richard Rued, his wife Dee, and their children have long ties to the Sonoma Valley, too. Richard—who pours wine in a cowboy hat and could give Clint Eastwood a run for his money in the rugged charm department—got his start as a grower and a rancher back in the 1950s, when

RUED WINES

3850 Dry Creek Road,
Healdsburg
Exit Dry Creek Road west
from Highway 101

Tel. 707.433.3261,
ruedvineyards.com

Tasting daily 11 a.m.
to 4:30 p.m.

he grew grapes and prunes as part of an agricultural project in high school. For a long while, the family turned its attention to raising cherries, beef, and hay just to the east in the Alexander Valley and on the property that great-granddad Rued was running as a vineyard from the 1880s until Prohibition shut him down.

Today, the family grows grapes on land in the Dry Creek, Alexander, and Russian River Valley AVAs, selling most of it on to other local winemakers. But since 2000 they have also been producing around four thousand cases a year of 100 percent estate-grown Cabernet Sauvignon, Sauvignon Blanc, Chardonnay, Pinot Noir, and Zinfandel wines in the $15 to $45 range. Their limited-production Sauvignon Blanc tastes like spring itself and recently took a gold at the *San Francisco Chronicle* International Wine Judging Competition.

UNTI VINEYARDS

4202 Dry Creek Road,
Healdsburg
Exit Dry Creek Road west
from Highway 101

Tel. 707.433.5590,
untivineyards.com

Tasting daily 10 a.m. to 4 p.m.
by appointment only

IF YOU START ASKING the locals for recommendations about whose wine you can't miss in the Dry Creek, one name that you'll keep hearing is Unti Vineyards. It's a testament to the friendly spirit of Sonoma winemakers and to the warm welcome that awaits visitors down at the end of this dusty back lane.

The family—George, Linda, and Mick—has been producing wines commercially since 1997, and the emphasis on northern Italian and southern French wines is a nod in two directions: to the Unti family's roots in Tuscany and to Mick's passion for the wines of Provence and the Côtes du Rhône. Besides, as Mick will tell you with a warm smile, the climate of the Dry Creek AVA is ideally suited to traditional Mediterranean varieties. Grapes like Grenache and Mourvèdre or Syrah and Montepulciano will someday become California favorites, he predicts. Unti Vineyards is leading the way in this delicious revolution.

Here, the emphasis isn't on a house style but on the expression of terroir—always with an international twist. With winemaker Sébastien Pochan, Mick makes somewhere on the order of seven thousand cases of estate reds, all grown in vineyards that have been farmed using sustainable and biodynamic techniques. Best of all, these are wines priced for the world market, and no one is asking you to pay inflated boutique prices. Their dry rosé (just over $20)—a Grenache Noir and Mourvèdre blend—was inspired by a trip to Nice, where this traditional Provençal wine is served at sidewalk bistros with pizza, and if I could have just one summer afternoon wine, this would be it. There is also a hearty

Zinfandel that could stand up to any steak on the grill, along with Syrah and their signature "Segromino"—a Sangiovese-led blend. Most wines are in the $20 to $40 range, and if you want a vineyard tour, just ask when you call for an appointment.

MONTEMAGGIORE

2355 West Dry Creek Road,
Healdsburg
Exit Dry Creek Road west
from Highway 101

Tel. 707.433.9499,
montemaggiore.com

Tasting by appointment only

THE CIOLINO FAMILY—Vincent, Lise, and their young son,
Paolo—trace their roots back to a small mountain village called
Montemaggiore Belsito in the Italian *mezzogiorno*, and they have
named their winery after it. On their mountain property here in
Sonoma's Dry Creek, they grow sustainably and biodynamically
farmed grapes and olive trees, and the result is some excellent
Syrah and artisanal oil. Vincent is the farmer in the family, and
Lise is the winemaker. They make only a few wines—a white, a
rosé of Syrah, a vineyard Syrah, and a reserve wine that in 2007
garnered points in the 90s from *The Wine Advocate*'s Robert
Parker (from $25 to $45). Because it's a small family operation,
you have to make an appointment to visit, but they are delighted
to welcome you out to the vineyard for a tour and a chance to
sample the wines that are making their reputation.

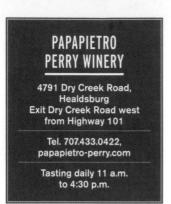

PAPAPIETRO PERRY WINERY

4791 Dry Creek Road,
Healdsburg
Exit Dry Creek Road west
from Highway 101

Tel. 707.433.0422,
papapietro-perry.com

Tasting daily 11 a.m.
to 4:30 p.m.

CLUSTERED TOGETHER up a steep driveway on the north side of Dry Creek Road are the tasting rooms and production facilities of nearly a dozen small family wineries, and one of the standouts is the Papapietro Perry Winery, home to some highly acclaimed Pinot Noir wines.

Friends and former newspapermen Ben Papapietro and Bruce Perry first got the idea of making their own wines after a weekend working the crush, and they spent much of the next two decades making wines, in the early days out in the garage using an old hand press. Although they only produced their first commercial vintage in 1998, they already have a world-class reputation, with accolades that include the 2007 *Wine Spectators*'s Critics Choice Award. The focus here is on Pinot Noir and Zinfandel wines in the $50 to $70 range, made from fruit sourced from the best small vineyards in the county. The tasting fee is $10.

RUN BY THE father-and-son team of Fred and Jamie Peterson, the Peterson Winery is a friendly, family affair. Their story started out in the vineyards, where Fred began by supplying grapes to local estates. These days, he says that he likes to think of himself still as a winegrower—someone growing fruit that will make a great wine. And at Peterson, where the philosophy is one of "zero manipulation," the character of the fruit and the land is pretty much everything.

PETERSON WINERY

4791 Dry Creek Road, Healdsburg
Exit Dry Creek Road west from Highway 101

Tel. 707.431.7568,
petersonwinery.com

Tasting daily 11 a.m. to 4:30 p.m.

These days, son Jamie is the winemaker, and, if you want to get some hands-on experience as part of your tasting adventure, Peterson offers some of the most intriguing special events in the county. Jamie occasionally offers wine-blending seminars (around $50, inquiries to friends@petersonwinery.com), where you can learn about how wine is structured and then blend and bottle your own special vintage for enjoyment back home.

But first you might want to try some of the wines Jamie has blended. The *San Francisco Chronicle* recently selected his Sangiovese as one of the year's top 100 wines, and other offerings range from Petite Sirah and Carignane wines to a couple of summer rosés and a dessert wine of vintage Muscat Blanc. There are also familiar favorites like Cabernet Sauvignon, Pinot Noir, and Sauvignon Blanc. Peterson Winery produces around four thousand cases a year of small-lot, handcrafted wines, in the $15 to $55 range, with many under $25.

HEADING DOWN THE LANE that leads to the tasting room at Talty, you drive right through the vineyards, and what you are looking at, Mike Talty will tell you, is the daily love and labor of a man who thinks of himself first and foremost as growing wine, not grapes.

Mike is dedicated to perfecting just one varietal: Zinfandel. His winery produces less than thirteen hundred cases a year and just three single-vineyard-designate wines—one an estate Zinfandel grown on the seven acres of property out front, one Dry Creek Zinfandel from fruit here in the AVA, and the other a Napa County Zinfandel made from grapes raised on a two-and-a-half-acre parcel he manages over on the other side of Sonoma Mountain.

The estate fruit on the property comes from fifty-year-old head-pruned vines, and this was all once part of one of the large ranches that used to cover the valley. Mike bought the parcel in the late 1990s and released the first Talty vintage in 2001. Almost immediately, he made his mark in the wine world when the estate Zinfandel was hailed by the *Wall Street Journal* as an undiscovered gem, and readers were advised to "remember the name of this Sonoma winery; you'll be hearing it."

But despite all this attention, Mike still keeps things down to earth at Talty Vineyards. It's the kind of place where the tasting bar is a piece of wood propped up on two old oak barrels and where the focus is on just one thing: great handmade wines in the $30 to $40 range.

TALTY VINEYARDS AND WINERY

7129 Dry Creek Road, Healdsburg
Exit Dry Creek Road west from Highway 101

Tel. 707.322.8438,
taltyvineyards.com

Tasting Friday to Monday noon to 4 p.m. and Tuesday to Thursday by appointment only

FOR DAVID COFFARO, it all began with Bordeaux. Working in finance down in San Francisco in the 1960s and 1970s, he soon found himself buying wine futures and building a collection. He still remembers with a smile the wine glut of 1970, when prices crashed. He filled his cellars and drank luxuriously for the better part of the next decade. By the early 1980s, David and his wife, Pat, left the city and purchased twenty-five acres of vineyards on the northern end of the Dry Creek Valley, taking their chances on building a winery in this still undiscovered corner of Sonoma County.

And at David Coffaro wines, it's still all about taking your chances. They produce around five thousand cases of wine a year, and, while you can buy from the bottled wines they have on hand when you visit the tasting room, a good part of their annual vintage is sold through what they call their "Crazy Back to the Futures" program—a chance for enthusiastic aficionados and collectors alike to purchase wines early in the season at what generally amounts to a 40 percent discount or more. It's your chance to pick up an estate wine that normally retails for $40 for under $25.

Because it's all about taking your best guess at what the future is going to bring, the lowest prices are available early in the season (usually April), and a visit to the tasting room generally means bellying up to the barrel. To take some of the guesswork out of it all, the folks at David Coffaro will help you understand exactly what is happening in the barrel and how a wine evolves, and you can always track the progress of the vintage online at

David's winemaker's diary (coffaro.com/diary.html). You can also take a peek at the impressive range of varietals grown in the vineyards and plot out some new tasting adventures. It's a fresh take on daily life in the wine business and a great way to keep tabs on what to expect from next year's bottles-to-be.

Unlike some other wineries with futures programs, David and Pat are flexible about when you pick up your wines, and they are happy to ship them if you live outside Sonoma County. Best of all, because David takes some calculated risks in his wine-making as well, you're likely to find some unique and delicious new blends. Zinfandel and Cabernet Sauvignon are the backbone on the vineyards, but here's also your chance to try—and maybe take an early gamble on—varietals that run the gamut from Barbera, Petite Sirah, and Carignane to Peloursin, Mourvèdre, Grenache, Petit Verdot, Tannat, Aglianico, or Lagrein. For all you dedicated wine lovers, it might just be more fun than a weekend in Las Vegas.

SBRAGIA FAMILY VINEYARDS

9990 Dry Creek Road,
Geyserville
Exit Dry Creek Road west
from Highway 101, north
of the Yoakim Bridge Road
intersection

Tel. 707.473.2992,
sbragia.com

Tasting daily 11 a.m. to 5 p.m.

IN THE CALIFORNIA wine industry, Ed Sbragia, who spent his career over in Napa as the head winemaker at Beringer, is something of a legend. Two of the wines he crafted—the 1986 Cabernet Sauvignon and the 1994 Chardonnay—were *Wine Spectator* wines of the year, and for more than thirty years lucky collectors around the world have made room for his handiwork in their cellars.

But making wine and honoring the family's roots in the Dry Creek Valley was also Ed's retirement dream. His grandfather came to California from the graceful little Italian city of Lucca in the first decade of the twentieth century and worked in the wineries. Father Gino eventually saved enough to buy some vineyards, and Ed grew up on the family ranch here in the valley. Even with a job over in Napa, this is where he raised his own kids. Where else would anyone find the Sbragia Family Vineyards?

For the past few years, Ed and his son, Adam, have been making wines under the new family label—a Dry Creek Chardonnay, Zinfandel, Sauvignon Blanc, Merlot, and Cabernet Sauvignon, plus a few Chardonnay and Cabernet wines made from some special grapes grown over in Napa. As you might expect, the response has been gleeful. The Gamble Ranch Chardonnay ranked number fifteen on *Wine Spectator's* Top 100 Wines list in 2007, and, for those who like to crunch the numbers, these are wines consistently ranked at 90 points or higher. The total production is just under six thousand cases a year, and someday they might go as high as ten thousand. But the idea is always to keep this a labor of love. The wines range from $20 to more than a $100, with most around $35.

The views from the hillside tasting room are spectacular. The Dry Creek Valley rolls out for miles on your left, and to the right is the monumental face of the Warm Springs Dam, which holds back the waters of Lake Sonoma. Tasting ranges from around $10 to $20 depending on the experience you opt for.

BELLA VINEYARDS AND WINE CAVES

9711 West Dry Creek Road,
Healdsburg
Exit Dry Creek Road west
from Highway 101, north
of the Yoakim Bridge Road
intersection

Tel. 866.572.3552,
bellawinery.com

Tasting daily 11 a.m. to
4:30 p.m.; cave and vineyard
tours by appointment only

AT THE VERY NORTHERN end of the West Dry Creek Road is the little tasting room at Bella Vineyards. The tasting experience—which takes place by candlelight in their echoing underground caves—is one of the most charming and atmospheric you'll find anywhere, and their late-harvest Zinfandel (around $25) is an excellent wine. In 2007 it took the double gold and best of class medals in the *San Francisco Chronicle* Wine Competition.

With a focus on small-lot, handcrafted wines, Bella puts the emphasis exclusively on reds, with several Zinfandels on offer, including Zinfandel and Petite Sirah blends and a couple of 100 percent varietal wines, sourced from the Dry Creek Valley and the nearby Alexander Valley AVAs. Those wines are award winning as well. In a recent ranking, three of their 2009 Zinfandel releases garnered points in the 90s. The price range is $25 to $40, and the tasting fee is $10. It's a beautiful and hopelessly romantic little spot with some wines that are definitely worth trying.

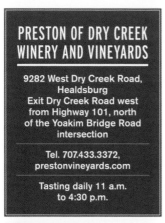

PRESTON OF DRY CREEK WINERY AND VINEYARDS

9282 West Dry Creek Road,
Healdsburg
Exit Dry Creek Road west
from Highway 101, north
of the Yoakim Bridge Road
intersection

Tel. 707.433.3372,
prestonvineyards.com

Tasting daily 11 a.m.
to 4:30 p.m.

WHEN SONOMA COUNTY locals have out-of-town visitors to entertain, there is one Dry Creek winery that everyone puts on the itinerary for the perfect wine country weekend: the rustic extravaganza that is the Preston family winery. It's located on the north end of the valley, down a long gravel road that runs along the creek and through ranch land. There is nothing pretentious about the life that Lou and Sue Preston have built here on property they bought back in the early 1970s. Yet you can't help but think that they've got it all here.

They make wine, of course. In fact, they make excellent wine, with an emphasis on food-friendly wines made from Italian and southern French varietals: Zinfandel, Petite Sirah, and Barbera lead among the reds, and among the whites there's a Vin Gris, a Sauvignon Blanc, and a white Rhône-style blend called Madame Preston. All the wines are reasonably priced, mostly in the $20 to $40 range, and it's a great chance to take your palate on a little trip to the south of France, Dry Creek style. The $10 tasting fee is refunded with the purchase of a bottle.

But, as everyone will tell you, wine is just part of the Preston experience. Lou makes what is generally acknowledged to be the best bread in the county, and you can buy warm loaves on the weekends. In the summer they run their own little farmers' market outside the front door of the winery, with sun-ripened heirloom produce grown right here on their organic farm and in their gardens. There are estate-cured olives and olive oils (around $30), pick-your-own strawberry patches, local cheese on sale, bocce ball courts where you can engage in a little spirited competition (open weekdays only), friendly farm cats looking for ankles to rub, and plenty of space for the impromptu picnic you are almost certain to end up enjoying here in this little corner of paradise.

STEVE ZICHICHI (pronounced Zoo-kiki), a New Orleans physician, had been dreaming of a move to the wine country for the better part of a decade when Hurricane Katrina came along. He and his wife, Kristin, were already avid wine collectors and had purchased twenty-two acres of land here in the Dry Creek Valley, a place they first discovered out wine tasting. After Katrina, they finally took the plunge, crafting their first vintage in 2004 and relocating to California with their four kids in 2006.

ZICHICHI FAMILY VINEYARDS

8626 West Dry Creek Road, Healdsburg
Exit Dry Creek Road west from Highway 101, north of the Yoakim Bridge Road intersection

Tel. 707.433.4410, zichichifamilyvineyard.com

Tasting daily; call for current hours

I discovered their Zinfandel during one of the big barrel-tasting weekends when local winemakers throw open their cellar doors in the spring. This is wine that tastes like the Dry Creek smells—of warm earth and fresh air. And this simple and intense expression of terroir is exactly the idea at Zichichi. The vineyards just beyond the tasting room were planted in the 1920s, and the secret to these wines is a simple one: great land, with great vines, and, Steve will tell you with a laugh, owners who have the good sense not to meddle with what nature has created.

The total production is around four thousand cases a year, with a focus on small-lot red wines, including two estate-grown Zinfandels, a Petite Sirah, and a Cabernet Sauvignon ($25 to $50). They've been selling out every year, so call ahead to find out what they are tasting and when the next release is coming. From the rustic tasting room, you've got long views over the Dry Creek Valley, and visitors are welcome to bring a picnic.

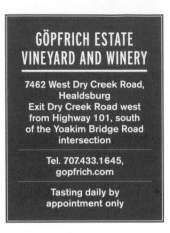

GÖPFRICH ESTATE VINEYARD AND WINERY

7462 West Dry Creek Road, Healdsburg
Exit Dry Creek Road west from Highway 101, south of the Yoakim Bridge Road intersection

Tel. 707.433.1645, gopfrich.com

Tasting daily by appointment only

WINE TASTING WITH Ray Göpfrich—the man behind the Göpfrich Estate Vineyard and Winery—is a convivial affair, where visitors settle in around a big wooden table and get a personal introduction to the 100 percent estate red wines made from fruit grown just out beyond the back door. The Göpfrich family came to Sonoma County in the early 1990s, when Ray retired from an academic career teaching dentistry, and, when they learned that the old vineyard on the property was too neglected to save, the new plantings were the Bordeaux- and Rhône-style varietals that thrive in the northern Dry Creek terroir. One of the fortunate results of this diverse vineyard is that, although Ray and his wife, Bonnie, make only six hundred cases of wine a year, there is an excellent range of things to try at Göpfrich.

There is a Zinfandel, of course. It's the signature wine of the Dry Creek Valley. But when I visited the winery, the folks gathered around were joking about turning "Ray Syrah Syrah" into a new ditty, and all the evidence pointed to an enthusiastic appreciation of his Syrah and his Syrah-Merlot Cuvée blend. A bit more unusually in the valley,

Göpfrich also produces a Cabernet Sauvignon, a consistent gold-medal winner in wine competitions, and, as Ray will tell you, because the Dry Creek Cabernets are less well known, they are one of the best values in the valley. Ray's estate reds are in the $30 to $40 range, and there's also a rosé on offer (around $20).

Before you get to these small-lot reds that have made the Göpfrich reputation, don't be surprised when you are offered another unique tasting experience. In homage to the family's German roots and to a long-standing friendship with an exchange student who lived with Ray and Bonnie in younger days, Ray also pours Rheinhessen wines from the Frank Klemmer family vineyards. These imported German whites (around $20)—as with all the wines at Göpfrich, available only in the tasting room or through direct winery sales—are aromatic and floral, and it's a great chance to try just one more family wine that you won't discover anywhere on the grocery store shelves.

RAYMOND BURR VINEYARDS AND WINERY

8339 West Dry Creek Road,
Healdsburg
Exit Dry Creek Road west
from Highway 101, south of
Yoakim Bridge Road

Tel. 888.900.0024,
raymondburrvineyards.com

Tasting daily 11 a.m. to 5 p.m.

RAYMOND BURR and Robert Benevides met back in the 1950s when they were actors on the *Perry Mason* show, and they went on to work again famously in *Ironsides*. But their most delicious partnership never had anything to do with Hollywood: their love of fine wines and rare orchids has been at the heart of the Raymond Burr Vineyards since the late 1980s.

Today, the solar-powered winery is named in memory of Burr, who passed away in 1993, and Robert Benevides continues to celebrate their shared passion for this Dry Creek estate and his family's Portuguese heritage. The wines on offer include award-winning Chardonnay, Cabernet Franc, and Cabernet Sauvignon in the $30 to $45 range, and visitors can also sample an estate port, made in the classical style, from Tinta Caõ, Tinta Madeira, and Toriga varietals (around $50).

Whatever you do, don't miss the orchid tour on the estate. It alone is worth the drive to this far end of the Dry Creek Valley. There are more than a thousand stunning varieties in these sultry greenhouses, and the blooms are nearly as intoxicating and fragrant as the wines. Visits are available by advance appointment only on Saturday and Sunday at 11 a.m., and it's a rare chance to be introduced to a world-class collection by a renowned expert and devoted enthusiast.

BEFORE THE SETTLEMENT of California and reaching back far into history, the Wine Creek was the site of a Native American fishing village and home to the Southern Pomo Indians. In recent centuries, this area was turned into ranches, orchards, and, of course, vineyards. Today, one corner of the Dry Creek Valley is home to the Martorana Family Winery, and their history has its roots in the story of Italian immigration to this region in the early part of the twentieth century.

Hailing from a family of winemakers, father-and-son team Tony and Gio Martorana have been growing grapes here in the Dry Creek Valley for more than thirty years. Today, Gio makes the wine ($25 to $45). The Zinfandel is their signature varietal, but the vineyards at Martorana are also planted to Cabernet Sauvignon, Merlot, Chardonnay, some Petite Sirah, and—just recently—some Sauvignon Blanc that they hope to start producing wine from soon. In fact, you can't miss the Petite Sirah plantings: they cover the side of the environmentally conscious winery. The building's roof is planted with sedums, which keep the building naturally cool without air-conditioning, and everything is done using organic farming practices.

Gio also produces an estate olive oil made from handpicked fruit, and a visit to Martorana is a slice of *la dolce vita*. There are walking trails that start just a hundred feet from the winery and wind along the Dry Creek. In spring, the bocce courts are filled with the heady scents of citrus blooms. After a private tasting (ask for current prices), you're invited to settle in and enjoy some good wine and the sunshine.

MOUNTS FAMILY WINERY

3901 Wine Creek Road,
Healdsburg
Follow West Dry Creek Road,
north of Lambert Bridge Road,
to Wine Creek Road

Tel. 707.292.8148,
mountswinery.com

Tasting by appointment only

THE MOUNTS FAMILY WINERY is what back lane wine tasting is all about. You follow the sign down a gravel track through the vineyards, and there you are on the doorstep of one of the Dry Creek's new wineries. The family dog is the cellar mascot; the owners, proprietors, and winemakers—Dave and Lana Mounts—live and work on this ranch.

Dave grew up in the vineyards, and his family has been growing grapes in Sonoma County for three generations on land that his father bought back in the 1940s. But the winery only got its start in 2005, and they have recently celebrated their first release of estate wines. The Mounts produce a select range of small-lot and handcrafted wines, focusing on Viognier, Grenache, Syrah, Petite Sirah, Zinfandel, Malbec, and Cabernet Franc varietals, in the $15 to $40 range, and this is one of the friendliest and most personal wine tasting experiences you'll find anywhere in the county.

THE FOLKS at A. Rafanelli Vineyard and Winery aren't always great about returning phone calls, and the tasting rooms are open only by appointment. But they've been making wines in the Dry Creek Valley for more than four generations, and they have one of the best reputations locally for making great red wines. Their Zinfandel is generally considered superior and emblematic of the Dry Creek AVA. In fact, most of these wines are so good there are limits on how many bottles you can buy in the tasting room—which is the only place outside a few high-end restaurants that you'll ever find them. With a total production of just over ten thousand cases a year and this kind of a reputation, you can pretty well imagine that these wines (most in the $45-and-up range) don't come cheap. They've been considered cult wines for years.

If you do manage to get an appointment it's absolutely worth the trip. The tasting room is up a long steep driveway lined with redwood trees, surrounded by terraced vineyards, and the rustic barn-style winery feels a world away from the glitz and glitter that you'll find in much of the wine country. This place is still very much a family-run operation, and the tasting appointments are intimate affairs. If you do get an appointment, make sure you're not late, because they won't keep your spot for more than a few minutes. And you can't use your credit card here, so if you plan to buy—and it would be crazy not to take home a least one bottle—be sure to hit the bank machine first (or bring your checkbook).

A. RAFANELLI VINEYARD AND WINERY

4685 West Dry Creek Road, Healdsburg
Exit Dry Creek Road from Highway 101, just north of the Lambert Bridge Road intersection

Tel. 707.433.1385, arafanelliwinery.com

Tasting daily 10 a.m. to 4 p.m. by appointment only

VINEYARD OF PASTERICK

3491 West Dry Creek Road
Exit Dry Creek Road west
from Highway 101, south of
the Lambert Bridge Road
intersection

Tel. 707.433.4655,
pasterickwine.com

Tasting daily by
appointment only

THERE HAVE BEEN GRAPES on the site of the Pasterick vineyards since the 1880s, and the family farmhouse once belonged to the folks who established one of Sonoma County's landmarks, the Dry Creek General Store (page 68). The vineyards today are more recent, planted especially by Gerry Pasterick so he could create his signature California-inflected Côte Rôtie blend. Here on ten steep hillside acres, Gerry—a generous man with a sparkling wit and a passion for terroir—grows enough Viognier and Syrah to produce five hundred cases a year of his complex and eminently quaffable wine. Each year there is just one release of estate Syrah (around $40), and recently Gerry has added to the lineup a Viognier white wine (around $30) and a rosé wine (around $25). The afternoon I visited him, he had just finished gluing labels on the bottles, and Pasterick is very much the kind of place where everything about winemaking is intimate and personal.

If you ever wanted a real education in terroir, this is the place to come. Gerry will take you out back and show you his two hills. Here in the Dry Creek, the vintners can watch the sun rise over Geyser Peak, and in the far distance you might catch a glimpse of Napa's Mount St. Helena. Three million years ago, both were active volcanoes, and the valley floor is still covered in places with iron-rich ash from prehistoric explosions. You can see it immediately when Gerry points to the pale red of his northern slope. To the south, the hill is brown. It's 120 million years of crushed bedrock. With a laugh, he'll tell you that his Côte Rôtie style was inevitable: in France, they distinguish between the blond and brown subappellations. He's got them both in his backyard. If you visit at harvest time, you can taste the difference soil makes. It's the same rootstock and the same vineyard practices. But these are different grapes. That is the essence of terroir.

The winemaker's tour also includes a walk through the stand of coastal redwood trees that runs along the back edge of the property amid seasonal waterfalls, and from there it's down into the meandering underground caves where the wines are produced and stored. And, of course, you'll taste the wine. It's full of red fruit jam and spices, and it's not something you're going to sample anywhere else.

DE LA MONTANYA ESTATE VINEYARDS AND WINERY

999 Foreman Lane,
Healdsburg
Exit Westside Road from
Highway 101, west onto Felta
Road to Forman Lane, under
the Westside Road overpass

Tel. 707.433.3711,
dlmwine.com

Tasting daily 11:30 a.m. to
4:30 p.m.; by appointment only
on weekdays

THE DE LA MONTANYA FAMILY has been working the land in Northern California for nearly two hundred years, and, in an era when the true California native is rumored to be an endangered species, they are justifiably proud of having seven generations of local experience behind them. Like so many of the old families in Sonoma County, Dennis and Tina De La Montanya still make a good part of their living selling the grapes grown on their property to the big commercial outfits. But with 15 percent of their crop they have recently started making some of the valley's most coveted wines. Getting into the tasting room here takes advance planning except on the weekends, when the doors are open to drop-by visitors. Pretty soon, in fact, there will be a waiting list for joining the wine club. The production is limited to around forty-five hundred cases a year, and club members buy almost all of it. There are no plans to expand production, and that means this is cult wine in the making.

There are lots of things going on at De La Montanya. Not only does the family make an astonishing thirty different wines—many of them medal winners at the Sonoma County Harvest Fair and in the *San Francisco Chronicle* competitions—but this is also a place where their wine club members get unique perks, something more than the standard 15 or 20 percent case discount. The "Pin Up" wine series boasts labels with glamorous images of sexy ladies in tasteful boudoir settings (and you've now had your R-rated warning). But these are no L.A. models.

Every year, wine club members who want to strut their stuff can enter the Halloween drawing and win the chance to raise a few eyebrows. Club members get exclusive invites to wine bashes and access to the guest cottage on the property. But the good causes and good clean fun never get in the way of making serious wines, with an emphasis on Pinot, Syrah, and Zinfandel varietals in the $20 to $50 range.

DRY CREEK GENERAL STORE

3495 Dry Creek Road, Healdsburg
Exit Dry Creek Road west from Highway 101, at the Lambert Bridge Road intersection

Tel. 707.433.4171, drycreekgeneralstore1881.com

Open Monday to Thursday 6:30 a.m. to 5:30 p.m., Friday and Saturday 6:30 a.m. to 6:30 p.m., Sunday 7:00 a.m. to 6:30 p.m.

FOR A FANCY LUNCH in the Dry Creek area, you'll need to head back toward Healdsburg, where gourmet pleasures await. Up in this rural far end of the county, many of the wineries have picnic grounds where you can settle in with a deli lunch and a bottle of something special, and the Dry Creek General Store—a landmark in the valley since 1881—is the perfect place to pick up all the fixings. You can order custom sandwiches or pick up a fresh baguette to enjoy with gourmet cheeses and local olives. There is also a breakfast menu if you can't wait to get started with your morning wine tasting adventures. If you don't want to open one of your recent vineyard finds, you'll also discover a large selection of Dry Creek wines and a shaded beer garden where you can relax over a cold pint. Or perhaps the quirky full-service bar is more your style: it's got a bit of the Wild West about it still and is a local favorite.

A GENERATION or two ago, before California became wine country and a small ranch could be sold to aspiring winemakers (and these days, increasingly, to out-of-town investors) for staggering sums of money, prune and peach orchards covered the Dry Creek Valley. Today, most of the orchards are gone, and the Dry Creek Peach and Produce stand is the last fruit farm in the area. If you have never tasted a peach warm off the tree in the Californian sunshine, you haven't ever really tasted a peach at all. Just the smell of them can leave you dizzy.

DRY CREEK PEACH AND PRODUCE

2179 Yoakim Bridge Road, Healdsburg
Exit Dry Creek Road west from Highway 101, at Yoakim Bridge Road

Tel. 707.433.8121, drycreekpeach.com

July and August, most weekends from roughly noon to 5 p.m.

The fruit at Dry Creek Peach and Produce is grown organically, and this family-run business specializes in selling fruit and homemade jam (along with a small selection of heirloom vegetables) at local farmers' markets and to some of the Bay Area's most renowned restaurants. But during most Saturday and Sunday summer afternoons in July and August, from about noon onward, more or less, you'll be able to find them at the store or in the orchards. You can stop for a glass of homemade lemonade and buy some of the most exquisite peaches you will find anywhere.

CHAPTER 2

ALEXANDER VALLEY

WINERIES

PROVISIONS

DIVERSIONS

Maps on pages viii–ix

NAMED AFTER THE NINETEENTH-CENTURY pioneer Cyrus Alexander, the Alexander Valley was once open ranch land. Today, the area is known for producing some of California's finest Cabernet Sauvignon, and along its back lanes you'll find numerous small family wineries and some of the county's best dining establishments. The AVA begins just north of Healdsburg, with its tree-lined plaza and boutique shops, and it runs further northward along Highway 101 beyond Cloverdale. But the most charming wine tasting route is to work your way south from Cloverdale, sampling your way down River Road, perhaps taking in the historic site of the Italian Swiss Colony in Asti, and picking up Highway 128—the main wine road of the Alexander Valley— in Geyserville. From the southern end of the appellation, you can continue driving through the Chalk Hill or Knight's Valley areas, where the scenery is lovely but there are fewer wine tasting opportunities.

PENDLETON ESTATE VINEYARDS AND WINERY

35100 Highway 128,
Cloverdale
Exit Highway 128 from
Highway 101, 5 miles north

Tel. 707.894.3732,
pendletonwines.com

Tasting by appointment only

THE OAT VALLEY is well off the beaten path, and the small winery that Michall and Jeannine Pendleton run out of their family home is the last winery in the Alexander Valley appellation before Sonoma County gives way to the cooler, foggier landscape of Mendocino. That means that this isn't the kind of place where you pop in quickly on your way to another couple of appointments in an afternoon. Here, you come to settle in for the sort of one-on-one wine experience that only a passionate small proprietor is going to be able to give you. And it's quite an experience. Driving up through the gates of the Pendleton estate, you find yourself wondering whether you've been whisked away to some countryside French château. Except that when you get to the main terrace of the house, perched at the top of a small, narrow valley, you realize that the views are 100 percent California.

The Pendleton family came to the Alexander Valley in the early 1990s with no clear intention of making wines and no family legacy in the industry behind them. Michall was working then as a fireman and not a vintner. In fact, Michall credits his passion for winemaking to his friend and mentor, David Coffaro (page 42), who makes some of the most highly regarded small-lot wines in the Dry Creek Valley. The winemaking here at Pendleton is clearly a labor of love. Michall makes about five hundred cases a year, and all the wines are completely handmade, right down to the month given over to harvesting the grapes on four and a half acres of estate vineyards.

Despite the small production, there is an impressive array of wines—and an even more impressive array of gold medals from the wine competitions. Of the forty-one wines that he's entered in competitions, forty have taken medals. Many of the wines work with Petite Sirah as a varietal, but there is also a Russian River Zinfandel and a Mourvèdre on offer. Most wines are in the $25 to $30 range, with the opportunity to barrel sample and order futures in the spring, and there is no charge for wine tasting. If you don't make it up to see Michall in person, you can also sample the Pendleton wines at the Locals tasting room (page 88) in Geyserville.

PEAY VINEYARDS

207A North Cloverdale
Boulevard, Suite 201,
Cloverdale
Vineyard directions provided
with appointment

andy@peayvineyards.com,
peayvineyards.com

Tasting by appointment only

EVERY YEAR, the *San Francisco Chronicle* gives the nod to one winery that the critics think is doing something really special. Not too long ago that winery of the year was Peay Vineyards.

This tiny, family-run operation—the brainchild of brothers Nick and Andy Peay; Nick's wife, Vanessa Wong; and Andy's wife, Ami—can do only a couple of tasting appointments a month, and you need to let them know weeks in advance. But if you're serious about your cool-climate wines and looking for a chance to add something unique to your cellar, their Pinot Noir is stellar. They make four different Pinot Noir wines, and the fruit comes from an organically farmed estate vineyard perched on a hilltop in the far northwestern corner of the county, where the ocean breezes shape the character of the terroir, and from a few other special vineyards in the area. They also make a limited production of estate Viognier and an estate Rousanne and Marsanne blend. Most wines are in the $45 to $55 range.

THE TIN CROSS VINEYARDS were first planted to vine by some intrepid homesteaders in 1855, and those early farmers had a good eye for the land. When May-Britt and Denis Malbec—whose background in the winemaking world includes Denis's time as cellar master at the legendary Château Latour in Bordeaux—first saw it, they

CAPTÛRE WINES

P.O. Box 1820, Healdsburg
Vineyard directions provided
with appointment

info@capturewines.com,
capturewines.com

Tasting by appointment only

knew this was the kind of terroir capable of producing something rare and world-class. Today, the vineyard is at the heart of the winemaking program at Captûre, which is owned by the Foster family, and the press is already sitting up and taking notice. In 2013 *Wine Spectator* named this a winery to watch. The wines—Bordeaux-style reds and whites, primarily Sauvignon Blanc, Chardonnay, and Cabernet Sauvignon—range from $30 to $140. There is no tasting room and only a limited number of appointments, but this is one of those ultimate back lane wineries for the serious aficionado.

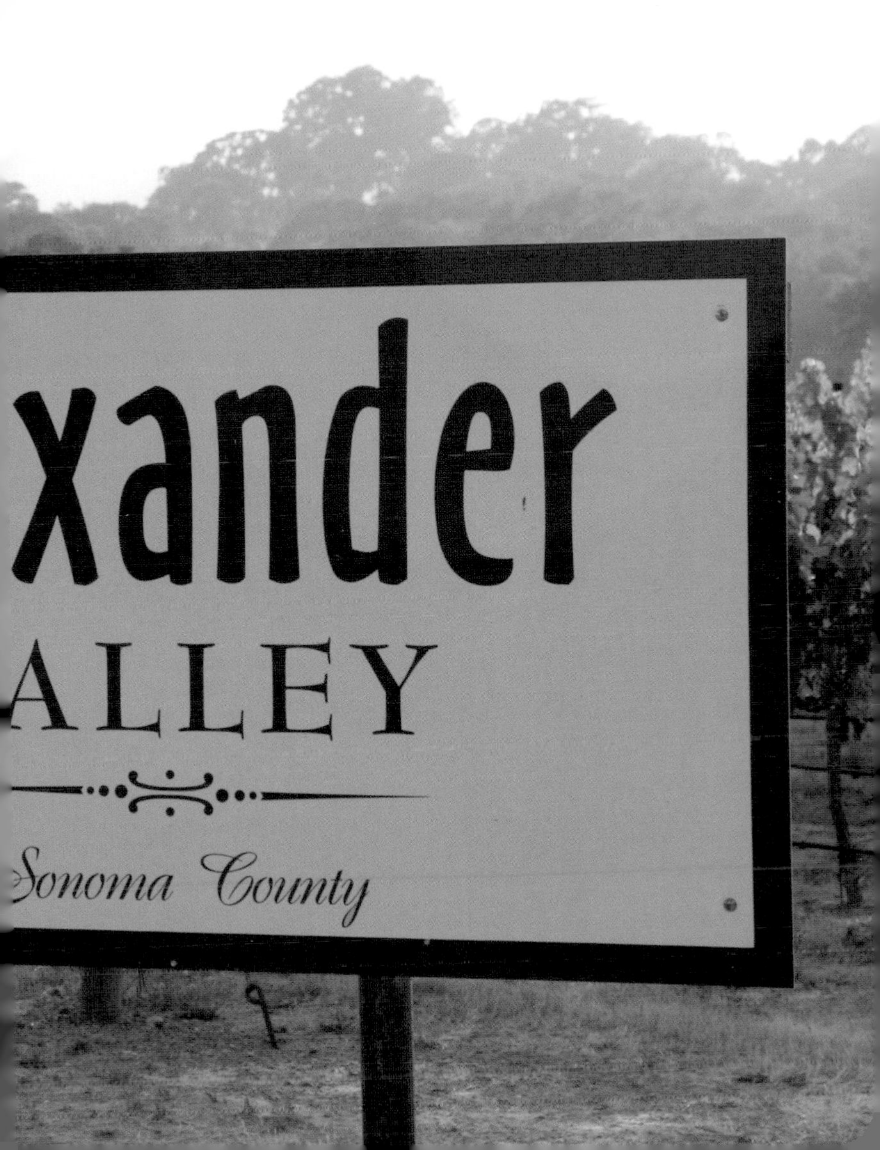
xander
ALLEY
Sonoma County

HAWKES WINERY

6734 Highway 128,
Healdsburg
Exit Highway 128 east from
Highway 101

Tel. 707.433.4295,
hawkeswine.com

Tasting daily 10 a.m. to 5 p.m.

IN THE LAST decades of the nineteenth century, the Alexander Valley was acre after acre of rugged ranch land, spread out along the small creeks that fill the Russian River to its banks (and sometimes more) come spring. The little stretch of Highway 128 north of Red Winery Road was once known simply as Jimtown, after James Patrick and the general store he ran there. Today, this settlement and the historic Victorian property that remains is home to another small family business, Hawkes Winery, run by Paula and Stephen Hawkes; their son, Jake, and their daughter-in-law, Laura.

Like so many of the area's small producers, the family worked for decades as growers in vineyards they have owned since the early 1970s, supplying high-quality fruit to prestigious premium labels like nearby Silver Oaks. The family has been making their own wine now for almost a decade and brings to it two generations of expertise and the passion of those who know and love the land. They make superb small-batch wines, made from 100 percent estate-grown fruit, with prices in the $20 to $65 range, and, if you get chatting at the tasting bar, Laura will proudly tell you that they got their own equipment not too long ago. Before that, they were crafting their three thousand–odd cases of Cabernet Sauvignon, Merlot, and Chardonnay a few miles down the road at one of the local cooperatives. These are wines worth putting down, and there's still time to discover them before the big-name critics do.

If you find yourself over in the other end of the valley, they also have a tasting room on Sonoma Plaza (page 222).

ROBERT YOUNG ESTATE WINERY

4960 Red Winery Road,
Geyserville
Northwest on Highway 128,
turn east on Red Winery Road

Tel. 707.431.4811,
ryew.com

Tasting daily 10 a.m. to
4:30 p.m.

THE YOUNG FAMILY has been farming this parcel of sprawling ranch land on the eastern side of the Alexander Valley since the late 1850s, when a certain Peter Young gave up looking for gold and settled down just outside the small community that would come to be known as Geyserville. Five generations later, the Young family—siblings Fred, Jim, JoAnn, and Susan—still farm this historic ranch, which has been the site of estate vineyards since the 1960s.

Today, when you arrive at the winery it still feels like you've stumbled across someone's much-loved family home. There's the old ranch house with its long veranda looking right out onto acres upon acres of vineyards that turn brilliant reds and oranges in the autumn after harvest. Over in the big white barn, in the shade of ancient oak trees, you'll find the small tasting room and the friendly staff.

And, of course, the wines are excellent. You can't make bad wine as a small proprietor and stay in business this long in Sonoma County. Their signature Bordeaux blend, "Scion," is particularly well regarded, and past vintages have been awarded a place on *Wine Enthusiast*'s Top 100 Wines list. They also produce Chardonnay and an estate-grown Merlot, along with smaller plantings in the vineyards of Pinot Blanc, Petit Verdot, Malbec, white Riesling, Cabernet Franc, Viognier, Sangiovese, and Melon de Bourgogne. The wines range from about $40 to $75, and the $10 tasting fee is refunded with purchase. The estate has some fine caves, but, if you want the winemaker's tour, you have to be sure to call in advance.

NORMA AND JOE RAMAZZOTTI started out in the fruit-growing business and years ago began turning out a few barrels of some homemade wine that quickly developed a passionate local following for its exceptional quality. Joe—born in Italy as Giuseppe—had a way with the vine that just came naturally. Inspired by the appeals to make more of the Ramazzotti vintage, in 2002

the couple finally took the plunge and opened up a winery here in the northern end of the Sonoma Valley, in the sweet but still out-of-the-way town of Geyserville. Along with Occidental and Graton, it's one of the quintessential back lane small villages of the wine country.

It's easy to miss their low-key tasting room on one of the main streets in Geyserville, too—but that would be a mistake. This is a friendly and leisurely place to visit, and you'll get a chance to sample the variety of the family's wines, which range from Chardonnay, white Riesling, Grenache Noir, and a dry Zinfandel rosé, to Barbera, Sangiovese, Cabernet Franc, and Italian-inspired blended wines. Best of all, they are one of the few producers in the county making a sparkling wine. There's a *blanc de noir*, and the fruit comes from the Dry Creek and North Coast regions. Wines range from around $20 to $40. The tasting fee is $5, waived with purchase.

SOMETIMES IN Sonoma County, rolling along the back lanes, you can still discover the next generation of winemaking talent before everyone else does. But the Garden Creek wines almost certainly aren't going to be a secret much longer. Only a few years after releasing their first vintage, Justin Miller and Karin Warnelius-Miller have already garnered national attention from *Wine Enthusiast* and *Savor* magazines. What caused all the fuss were just a couple hundred cases of their hand-crafted Bordeaux-style red known as "Tesserae" (around $70). The name comes from the word for the small pieces of broken tile that are used to create a mosaic, and this harmonious combination of elements is the essence of the house philosophy here at Garden Creek. Currently, production is limited to this premium Cabernet Sauvignon blend and to two hundred cases of estate Chardonnay.

Even though Garden Creek is a new enterprise, Justin and Karin come to winemaking with a lifetime of experience. Karin grew up locally, in the middle of vineyards planted with old Italian-style varietals. Justin's family has owned the one hundred acres here on the Garden Creek ranch since the 1950s, and he was running the vineyards at eighteen. The thing you notice on first meeting them is a hands-on style born of experience. A visit to Garden Creek starts with the scents of wisteria and redwood over in the winery. Justin milled the boards for the building. In fact, 50 percent of the building materials came from reclaimed sources, and it's all solar-powered. It's the same in the vineyards.

The couple farms the ranch using organic and biodynamic techniques, composting even the wastewater from the winemaking process and hand-thinning the vineyards during the hot, dry summers in order to achieve maximum quality and consistency.

If all this sounds like a lot of hard work, don't let it give you the wrong idea. This is also one of those places where the natural beauty draws you into its own quiet rhythms. The creek bubbles softly in the background, and in mid-May peonies come tumbling out of the fences. You gather around an old oak barrel by candlelight for a taste of wine and some local gourmet nibbles in the cellars. Back out in the sunlight, there's the long view of the valley and the hillside olive groves, where by special request you can settle in for a wine-maker's luncheon and get a hands-on lesson in understanding terroir and the Bordeaux style. Tasting fees start at $25 for a wine-and-cheese pairing.

LOCALS

21023A Geyserville Avenue,
Geyserville
Exit Geyserville north
from Highway 101

Tel. 707.857.4900,
tastelocalwines.com

Tasting daily 11 a.m. to 6 p.m.

WISHING NOW you'd make made it out to the Dry Creek Valley to taste some of the Peterson family wines (page 37), but thinking it's too late? Or some of the Ramazzottti wines (page 85)? Or the wines of Eric Ross (page 201) or Michall Pendleton (page 74)? All is not lost. Even this far north, Sonoma County is still the Bay Area, and Locals is the valley's signature wine country cooperative. In fact, it was the first tasting room cooperative licensed in California, and it's a Sonoma County tradition. Carolyn Lewis and her staff pour wines for ten or so of the area's small-lot wineries (most in the $15 to $40 range), and this is the place to come if it's insider knowledge you're after—anything from restaurant recommendations to help contacting one of the families for a winemaker's tour. The wineries pouring at Locals change periodically, so there's always a new back lane discovery.

OWNED BY the Staten family for more than thirty years, Field Stone Winery is the kind of place that inspires loyalty from its local fans. When I was last there, a couple from down the road was picking up a mixed case for their cellar and making an afternoon of it. And given its reputation for producing some of the Alexander Valley's highest quality wines, it's no wonder. Legendary wine critic Robert Parker applauds Field Stone as "a consistent producer of one of California's better Sauvignon Blancs," and their Merlot, Cabernet Sauvignon, and Petite Sirah wines (most in the $20 to $40 range) have all been recent gold medal winners. With a wine list that includes Italian and Rhône varietals, along with more familiar grapes, this is also a good place to branch out and experience a California-style Sangiovese or the increasingly popular white Viognier.

But what's best about Field Stone—like so many of the genuinely family-run small wineries of Sonoma County—is their accessibility. Always wanted to do a barrel tasting? As long as you call in advance, the folks at Field Stone would be more than happy to oblige, whatever time of year you are visiting. After all, it only means walking into the front room. Visitors to the winery walk past a room of stacked oak barrels, with that sweet woody aroma, on the way to the tasting room. It's another one of those working wineries where you can learn about the craft from those who love it best.

FIELD STONE WINERY

10075 Highway 128,
Healdsburg
North of the Highway 128 and
Chalk Hill Road intersection

Tel. 800.544.7273,
fieldstonewinery.com

Tasting daily 10 a.m. to 5 p.m.

JIMTOWN STORE

6706 State Highway 128,
Healdsburg
Exit Highway 128 east from
Highway 101

Tel. 707.433.1212,
jimtown.com

Serving Monday, Wednesday,
Thursday 7:30 a.m. to 3 p.m.;
weekends 7:30 a.m. to 5 p.m.;
closed Tuesday

ALTHOUGH THE JIMTOWN STORE has been a local landmark in the Alexander Valley since the 1890s, when James Patrick started selling provisions to his fellow pioneers, the place is more than just a Sonoma County tradition. It's one of the great small American roadside cafés. And it's hardly undiscovered. You might have read about it in the pages of the *New York Times* or *Gourmet*.

But for all that, this is still a down-home country place, where you're just as likely to find the locals swapping the news as out-of-towners stopping by to pick up the fixings for that perfect picnic. You can preorder box lunches in the morning (call or order online) if your tasting agenda is particularly busy, or you can just stop by anytime to be tempted by some delicious home-cooked sweets and steaming good coffee while you wait.

You'll also find as you're browsing a good supply of local wines and local products, and on the first Thursday of the month there are special tasting events in the wine bar, where you can try wines from a rotating selection of back lane wineries. Best of all for you last-minute shoppers, it is the perfect place to pick up a hostess gift if you've been lucky enough to have friends driving you around all weekend. There are also Americana-inspired country toys for the kids back home, antiques for any of the grown-ups who are hankering for souvenirs, and the kind of charming vintage atmosphere that makes you wonder whether it really wasn't better in the good old days.

FOR CHEF AND OWNER Dino Bugica, pure and simple Italian cooking is a passion, and at Diavola it shows. This is the place to come at the northern end of the Sonoma wine country if all that wine tasting has made you hungry (or a bit lightheaded). There's a shady patio, classic and casual Italian food (entrées around $15 to $25) made with premium fresh ingredients, and a local wine list that has many favorite back lane reds by the glass.

DIAVOLA PIZZERIA AND SALUMERIA

21021 Geyserville Avenue, Geyserville
Exit Geyserville north from Highway 101

Tel. 707.814.0111,
diavolapizzeria.com

Serving daily 11:30 a.m. to 9 p.m.

There are pizzas cooked on the wood-burning oven, homemade sausages, panini, and pasta, and plenty of antipasti and fresh salads. There's nothing not to love about the place.

AMAZINGLY FOR A one-horse town, Geyserville is lucky enough to have two excellent Italian restaurants, and the second is Catelli's, run by owner and chef Nick Catelli and his wife, Domenica. The press has let the secret out of the bag, so it's often busy, and a reservation is recommended if you get a chance, but don't let that stop you from popping in to see if you get lucky. The food is Italian home cooking, with an emphasis on fun twists on *nonna*'s comfort dishes (the meatball sliders appetizer is a Geyserville legend). Their local calamari, kale salad, and rustic soups are other perennial favorites (entrées about $15 to $25), and for dessert there's everything from authentic gelato to a brownie sundae. And, what back lane wine tasters will really love? There's no corkage fee for any wine you bought in Sonoma County.

CATELLI'S

21047 Geyserville Avenue, Geyserville
Exit Geyserville north from Highway 101

Tel. 707.857.3471, mycatellis.com

Serving Tuesday to Thursday 11:30 a.m. to 8 p.m., weekends 11:30 a.m. to 9 p.m., Sunday noon to 8 p.m.

ITALIAN SWISS COLONY

Driving along the back lanes of the wine country, you will soon discover that there is no shortage of Italian names, and many of these immigrant families helped the wine industry in California flourish at the end of the nineteenth century. In fact, wine tasting in Sonoma County is nothing new. As early as the 1890s, scenic trains were carrying tourists up from San Francisco for winery tours and picturesque views of the vineyards.

The one place these early tourists had on their itinerary was the Italian Swiss Agricultural Colony. Established by Andrea Sbarboro in 1881 in the newly named town of Asti, just south of Cloverdale, the colony was part of the nineteenth-century American progressive vision. Here, unemployed Italian immigrants would be given work in the vineyards at wages of $30 a month, plus all the wine a man could drink, and the chance to purchase the land with part of their labor. But the workers were suspicious, and the community was soon converted to a joint-stock company.

By the 1920s that company, the Italian Swiss Colony Winery, had grown to the largest winery in the world and produced Asti's familiar sparkling wines, a range of old-style Italian varietals, and the bestselling "Tipo Chianti," the wine that made those rustic straw-covered bottles popular in America. During the 1960s, following the popularity of the Colony's "Little Old Winemaker, Me" advertising campaign, it had become the most visited tourist attraction in California after Disneyland. This was where the tasting room experience really got its start. Visitors were taken on winemaker tours through the cellars and the vineyards as a prelude to some serious sampling.

Beringer purchased the site of the historic vineyards back in the 1980s, and in 2008 the landmark winery was reopened briefly as part of the Cellar No. 8 brand at Asti Winery (cellarno8.com). The name is a nod to the original cellar, still standing, where the red wines were aged more than a century ago. Unfortunately, the historic site is once again closed to the public, though the wines are widely distributed. Curious history buffs, however, can still view California Historical Landmark #621 for the Italian Swiss Colony at the corner of Asti Road and Asti Post Office Road.

CHAPTER 3

HEALDSBURG

WINERIES

PROVISIONS

Maps on pages x–xi

ONCE PART OF AN INDIAN VILLAGE set in the midst of an ancient oak and madrone forest, the site of modern Healdsburg was known by the native Pomo people as Kale. By the1840s this entire area was part of a vast ranch deeded to Captain Henry Delano Fitch. In the 1850s a settler named Harmon Heald chose his favorite spot in the middle of another man's land, built a rustic squatter's cabin, and set up shop in a little trading post known as Heald's Store.

Today, Healdsburg remains true to its early commercial roots. Its shady, tree-lined plaza is ringed with some of the wine country's cutest boutique shopping. Café tables and sunny bistros entice you at every turn. And, of course, tasting rooms are tucked along alleys where you can discover new vintages crafted by talented small proprietors. Healdsburg is also the gateway to the Dry Creek Valley AVA and your best bet for local accommodation or a leisurely lunch. In addition to the excellent restaurants in town, Healdsburg hosts what is arguably the best farmers' market in all of Sonoma County on Saturday mornings.

HAWLEY WINERY

36 North Street
Exit Central Healdsburg north
from Highway 101, one block
north of the plaza

Tel. 707.473.9500,
hawleywine.com

Tasting daily 11 a.m. to 6 p.m.;
winery tours by appointment
Monday to Saturday 11 a.m.
to 4 p.m.

THE HAWLEY TASTING ROOM and gallery—run by John Hawley, his sons Paul and Austin, and Paul's wife, Meghan—is the Healdsburg outpost of the family's pastoral estate winery on Bradford Mountain over in the Dry Creek Valley. If you want the tour of the twenty-acre estate property and a chance to stroll through the vineyards with a winemaker, all you have to do is ask, and the family would be delighted to show you this special little corner of Sonoma. (If you do go, be sure to ask John about his passion for falconry and the hawks that still soar above the valley.)

If you're like most visitors to the wine country, you'll fall in love with Healdsburg and its impossibly quaint plaza, and it's no surprise that in recent years many of the local wineries have set up tasting rooms and salons in town, where you can stroll through the shops, sample wines, and find lots of choices for an excellent dinner. One place you won't want to miss on that itinerary is a visit to Hawley.

Dad John Hawley made his reputation as a winemaker with some of the area's most prestigious commercial estates and was one of the innovators behind the move to barrel fermentation in Sonoma County. He talks with the easy confidence of expertise about everything from the chemistry of a wine's bouquet to the advantages of sustainable agriculture. The family vineyards are certified organic—why use pesticides when the local wildlife is content to feast on the wild strawberries and tender weeds that grow underneath the vines? The boys, who grew up in the vineyards and learned their craft the old-fashioned way, are happy to show you firsthand what winemaking looks like and, of course, to give you a taste of the wines. Mom Dana Hawley is an artist, and her works (danahawley.com) adorn the walls of the downtown gallery. She paints vibrant and beautiful landscapes of this same valley where her husband and sons spend their days, and one of her creations might just be that perfect souvenir you're looking for. Son Paul is a filmmaker and photographer—and responsible for many of the back lane images you're currently enjoying.

The emphasis at Hawley is on French-style wines made from classic varietals such as Viognier, Chardonnay, Pinot Noir, and Cabernet Sauvignon, in the $20 to $45 range, and many are award winning. There's also a Dry Creek Zinfandel wine and late-harvest Zinfandel varietal that is a fabulous dessert selection. With a total estate production at right around three thousand cases a year, however, distribution of Hawley wines is limited. Tasting is $5.

SELBY WINERY

215 Center Street
Exit Central Healdsburg north
from Highway 101, south of
the plaza

Tel. 707.431.1288,
selbywinery.com

Tasting daily 11 a.m. to
5:30 p.m.

DOWN ONE OF THE little side streets that lead off the Healdsburg Plaza you can find the tasting room for Selby Winery, set in a green cottage covered with flowering vines. It's an intimate and friendly setting where you can sample some of Susie Selby's award-winning wines. In the world of women winemakers, she is one of Sonoma County's most talented.

Here in the wine country, the proprietors of small estates usually have one of two stories to tell. Either they come from families that have grown grapes in Northern California for generations, or they are newcomers who somewhere along the way fell in love with making wine and this luminous little corner of the world and decided to start again. The Selby story is one of the latter. Susie left a career in corporate America to learn the wine business from the cellar up with her dad, David, who passed away in 1997.

Now, Selby Winery produces on the order of twelve thousand cases a year of Russian River Valley and Sonoma County wine, and there is something here to suit every taste. Her Sauvignon Blanc recently took a gold medal in the Sonoma County Harvest Fair, and at just around $15 it has got to be one of the best bargains in the wine country. It's as good as wines that you'll pay twice as much for. Susie also makes a Syrah and a rosé of Pinot Noir that is wonderfully dry and drinkable, along with an old-vine Zinfandel, a Pinot Noir, and an award-winning Merlot that took honors at the 2007 National Women's Wine Competition. And she has recently introduced a great sparkling wine that is perfect for impromptu celebrating. Most wines are in the $15 to $45 range.

PORTALUPI WINE COMPANY

101 North Street
Exit Central Healdsburg east
from Highway 101, just north
of the plaza

Tel. 707.395.0960,
portalupiwine.com

Tasting daily 11 a.m. to 7 p.m.

THE HUSBAND-AND-WIFE team of Jane Portalupi and Tim Borges are the heart and soul of this little winery. They met growing up together in the same small town here in Northern California, and this is a love story that has had wine at the heart of it for decades. Today, they have a small production of special wines, sourced from fruit in Sonoma and in some of the other nearby wine areas that are just a bit less famous.

The tasting room is a relaxed, family-style environment where you can lounge at the tasting bar or settle into an armchair for a well-deserved wine country breather. They also offer the chance to book a private wine-education experience ($25), where the tasting is paired with local salami and cheese, and, if you request in advance, you can get a chance to talk to the winemaker, Tim Borges. He's the man behind the excellent Portalupi wines, which include a white blend and a port dessert wine as well as Zinfandel, Barbera, and Pinot Noir varietals (most wines around $20 to $50). If you're local—or if you want to live like one during your time in the wine country—pick up a gallon milk jug of their red blend (around $50), which is the perfect thing for beautiful everyday drinking.

IN RECENT YEARS a number of great family tasting rooms have sprung up along the bluff above the Russian River, which winds in a crook just east of the Healdsburg Plaza. Once an industrial area that was falling into disuse, the area around Front Street is now enjoying a renaissance and has become one of the hippest wine tasting areas in Sonoma. After all, airy loft spaces are the perfect place for wineries and hands-on tasting rooms.

SKEWIS WINES

57 Front Street
Exit Central Healdsburg
from Highway 101, east to
Healdsburg Avenue, north to
Front Street

Tel. 707.431.2160,
skewis.com

Tasting Saturday and Sunday
11 a.m. to 5 p.m. and by
appointment

One of the best small producers is Skewis, the purpose-driven artisanal winery founded by Hank and Maggie Skewis with just one objective: amazing Pinot Noir (around $50). They focus on pure varietal expression and low yields, using fruit sourced from Mendocino and Sonoma's Russian River Valley and Sonoma Coast AVAs, and their case production is tiny. This is wine that will make you understand, if you don't already, why the Pinot Noir from Northern California has an international reputation.

DAVIS FAMILY VINEYARDS

52 Front Street
Exit Central Healdsburg
from Highway 101, east to
Healdsburg Avenue, north to
Front Street

Tel. 707.433.3858,
davisfamilyvineyards.com

Tasting Thursday to Sunday
11 a.m. to 5 p.m.

ONE OF MY FAVORITE places for wine tasting in Sonoma County is the Davis Family Vineyards, run by the husband-and-wife team of Guy and Judy Davis. If you're looking for a place to spend a couple of hours on a warm spring afternoon, this riverside tasting room has a lot to offer. There is a shaded patio deck overlooking the Russian River, where you can take in the bucolic views, a bocce ball court where you can get down to some friendly competition, picnic tables, wines by the glass, music, and food-truck eats. The vegetables you'll find yourself enjoying were likely grown right here in the organic garden. This is a verdant retreat from all the pressures of a hard day's wine tasting.

The atmosphere is playful and lighthearted—but the wines are serious. The wines are Guy's passion, and the critics consistently recognize these as something special. His 2005 Syrah was named by *Wine & Spirits* magazine as one of the top twenty-five releases of the year, and there isn't a single one of his offerings that isn't award winning.

These are handcrafted wines that are true to the earth and to a sense of place, made with precision and a light touch. There is a Russian River Chardonnay and a small production of rosé made with Syrah and Viognier, a Zinfandel and a Zinfandel port, and of course the Russian River Pinot Noirs that have made Guy one of Sonoma County's most respected vintners. The wines are in the $20 to $50 range; tasting is $10, refunded with your purchase of a bottle.

VALDEZ FAMILY WINERY

113 Mill Street
Exit Central Healdsburg
east from Highway 101,
just south of the plaza

Tel. 707.433.3710,
valdezfamilywinery.com

Tasting Thursday to Sunday
11 a.m. to 5 p.m.

ULISES VALDEZ is one of those California success stories that remind you why you love the wine country. Ulises came from Mexico when he was sixteen to start farming in the vineyards of the Dry Creek Valley. (Many of those who work in the vineyards of Northern California are migrant laborers still, and, if you're interested in the history, local author Jonah Raskin spent a year working as a laborer for his memoir *Field Days: A Year of Farming, Eating, and Drinking Wine in California*, which is great travel reading.)

Ulises ultimately gained citizenship and convinced the man who gave him his first job in America to make him a partner in his vineyard management company. Today, in his forties, he runs with his wife and, increasingly, with his children, one of the most respected vineyard management firms in Sonoma County. In fact, he's something of a local legend. No one quite understands how or why, but people who know him joke that Ulises has ten green thumbs. It's the reason some of the most famous names in the valley have turned to him to farm the grapes in their vineyards, relying on his crew to prune the vines and drop fruit and harvest.

But Ulises also grows some grapes himself, and he's recently founded his own family label and opened a new tasting room just south of Healdsburg Plaza, where you can get a taste of what happens out there in the vineyards. These are wines that are an expression of the land that Ulises farms (many are vineyard-designated), and the winemakers are often friends—friends who also happen to be pretty famous vintners. There's a Pine Mountain Cabernet Sauvignon and a Silver Eagle Syrah, along with several great Zinfandel offerings, including the special St. Peter's Church Zinfandel. It's grown from historic grapes that were planted in a churchyard before Prohibition and that went on to become one of the most popular Zinfandel clones in Sonoma thanks to Ulises's work restoring the vineyard. The wines are in the $40 to $50 range mostly, and the emphasis is on excellent red varietals.

STARK WINE COMPANY

439 Healdsburg Avenue
Exit Central Healdsburg
east from Highway 101,
just north of the plaza

Tel. 707.431.8023,
starkwine.com

Tasting daily noon to 6 p.m.

STARK WINE COMPANY got its start—at least in the imagination—one weekend when Christian Stark and his then-girlfriend, Jen, took a trip to the wine country. Back in those days Christian was a rock-and-roll drummer and a culinary-school graduate, and he and Jen both fell in love with Healdsburg—something no visitor to the quaint and bustling little town will have any trouble understanding. A month later they moved, and Christian started out by working the harvest with winemaker David Georges at the celebrated Davis Bynum Winery. From there, he worked the harvest and production for a number of the Dry Creek Valley's best producers, including Unti Vineyards (page 28), Ridge Vineyards, and Bella Vineyards (page 46). By 2003, Christian and Jen were married and he was making his own wine, all with an eye toward someday founding their own family label.

Today, drawing on Christian's experience both as a cook and as a winemaker, Stark Wine Company produces about one thousand cases of food-friendly wine that is lighter on the oak and that emphasizes some of the less well-known varietals in the Rhône tradition. The fruit for some of the whites is sourced from small vineyards with exceptional terroir outside Sonoma County, and the Grenache Blanc and Viognier are great examples of why the Santa Ynez Valley and the Sierra foothills of California have growing reputations. Locally, there is also a vibrant Pinot Noir from the Russian River Valley and some wonderful reserve Chardonnay wines—if you can get them. These are wines made without a lot of fining, new blends are always in the works, and for Christian it's always about the unique expression of place.

Christian and Jen have a new tasting room, just a minute's walk from the northwest corner of the Healdsburg Plaza, and it's open for drop-ins daily. And it's not just a tasting room—it's also downtown Healdsburg's only bonded winery, where you can get a glimpse of what small-lot production looks like up close and personal. The wines range from $25 to $45, and the tasting fee is $10.

SEGHESIO FAMILY VINEYARDS

700 Grove Street
Exit Dry Creek Road east
from Highway 101, south
on Grove Street

Tel. 707.433.3579,
seghesio.com

Tasting daily 10 a.m. to 5 p.m.

THE STORY OF the Seghesio family is, in many ways, the story of winemaking in Sonoma County in microcosm. This is a fourth-generation Italian family winery, originally founded in 1895 by Edoardo Seghesio and his young wife, Angela. Edoardo came to California from his native Piedmont and found employment at the historic Italian Swiss Colony in Asti (page 94), becoming the winemaker and eventually raising enough money to buy fifty-six acres of ranch land in the northern reaches of the Alexander Valley. Soon, that ranch land was planted to Zinfandel, and, as the winery grew, Edourado acquired another ten acres of vineyards that were planted to old Chianti-style field blends. Today, those fields boast the most ancient Sangiovese plantings in California and some rare old-vine Barbera.

By the twentieth century, the Seghesio Family Vineyards was big business, and as late as the 1990s the company was producing more than 125,000 cases of wine a year, including their signature Zinfandel and Italian blends. Then, about fifteen years ago, the family decided it was time to consider a new direction. With some of Sonoma County's most storied vineyard holdings, the next generation at Seghesio was determined to give the land its fullest expression and to focus on producing premium wines in small, handcrafted lots.

Today, the total production has been limited to thirty thousand cases a year, making this one of the largest back lane family wineries in the county, and they are crafting an excellent range of

Zinfandel wines, as well as a Cabernet Sauvignon blend, select Barbera, Pinot Grigio, Pinot Noir, and Sangiovese releases, and what is still the wine country's only Arneis—crafted from a rare Italian grape perfectly suited to the Sonoma County terroir. The wines run from about $25 to $60, and the beautiful roadside tasting rooms feature a bocce ball court and sprawling picnic grounds where you are welcome to contemplate the good life at your leisure.

WILLIAMSON WINES

134 Matheson Street
Exit Central Healdsburg east
from Highway 101, southeast
end of the plaza

Tel. 707.433.1500,
williamsonwines.com

Tasting daily 11 a.m. to 7 p.m.

THE BEST PART of exploring the back lane wineries of Sonoma is getting the chance to talk one-on-one with the passionate and talented small proprietors who are living out their dreams in the vineyards and making some great wine. If that's the best part, second best has got to be finding a wine that is priced at about half of what it should be. These are wineries where the entire production sells out every year, and the only marketing is a classy tasting room and a sign outside the door. At Williamson Wines, this isn't just an accident—it's the house philosophy. When you get chatting with Bill Williamson, who runs the family winery along with his wife, Dawn, he'll tell you with a grin that the only people he wants to deal with are the folks who drink his wine. There's no advertising, no distribution, just three thousand cases a year of handcrafted small-lot wines and a dedication to giving visitors a memorable wine tasting experience.

Bill and Dawn Williamson came to Sonoma County in the early 1990s, but they both grew up in Australia, where Bill spent his summers out in the family vineyards. Bill didn't return to the wine business until later in life, after a successful entrepreneurial career in the software industry that took him from Sydney to California's Silicon Valley. There was never a time, he will assure you, when he didn't love wine. In fact, he saw all the business travel as a great opportunity to train his palate.

It's knowledge he's happy to share. The focus of the tasting experience at Williamson Wines is on finding simple and elegant ways to heighten your enjoyment of wine, and there is a nice array of wines to sample—everything from an easy and approachable Bordeaux-style Cabernet Sauvignon to Chardonnay, a sparkling wine, and a Shiraz. Every wine they have ever released has won a medal, despite the fact that with a small case production Bill and Dawn prefer not to enter many of the industry's biggest (and more expensive) wine contests. The wines are in the $30 to $125 range, and you can either stop by for a casual tasting at the bar or you can make an appointment for one of Bill's special "epicurean" dinners, where you'll get the chance to taste the Williamson wines over dinner in the company of a local star chef and the winemaker (around $150 per person). If you're looking for a big splurge and want to visit the wine country like a millionaire, ask about Bill's helicopter tasting tours, which are a completely unique perspective on the valley.

DOWNTOWN BAKERY AND CREAMERY

308A Center Street
Exit Central Healdsburg east
from Highway 101, eastern
side of the plaza

Tel. 707.431.2719,
downtownbakery.net

Serving weekdays 6 a.m.
to 5:30 p.m., Saturday 7:30
a.m. to 5 p.m., Sunday 7 a.m.
to 4 p.m.

ON SATURDAY MORNINGS in the summer, the ultimate wine country experience is wandering through the Healdsburg farmers' market, where local chefs give cooking demonstrations and the fresh flowers come falling out of the stalls in fragrant waves of color. The only thing that could possibly make it better is a creamy cappuccino and some truly delicious little breakfast pastry to enjoy while you are walking. My weekend ritual always involves a stop at the Downtown Bakery and Creamery. They make fresh breads every morning from locally milled flours, croissants from Sonoma County butter, and a dizzying array of homemade pastries that are often still warm from the ovens. In the afternoons, this is also the place to pick up a baguette for your picnic lunch, a fancy fruit tart for that dinner at a friend's house, or some homemade ice cream just to keep you going, and there is always steaming tea or coffee on offer.

JUST OFF Healdsburg Plaza there is a local favorite that it would be foolish to pretend is an undiscovered secret. When what you want is a gourmet sandwich for lunch or some fixings for an impromptu picnic, the Oakville Grocery is the obvious place to stop. The proprietors have gathered together on the store shelves all that is rare and delicious in Sonoma County, and you can find everything from cured olives to local cheese and charcuterie at the gleaming glass-cased deli counter. There's a shaded patio out front where you can enjoy hot sandwiches made to order (around $10), or you can order picnic box lunches in advance if you prefer not to build your own.

OAKVILLE GROCERY

**124 Matheson Street
Exit Central Healdsburg east
from Highway 101, southeast
corner of the plaza**

Tel. 707.433.3200,
oakvillegrocery.com

**Serving daily 9:30 a.m.
to 5 p.m.**

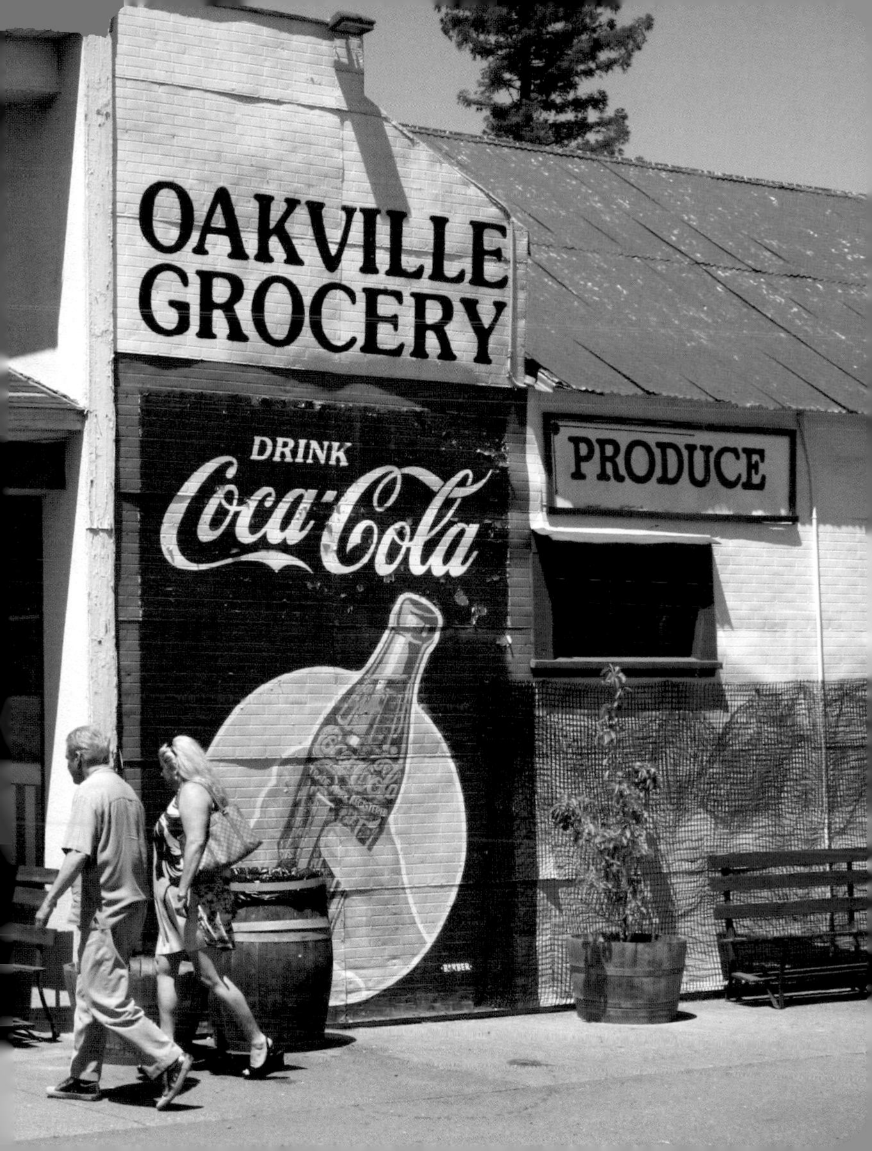
OAKVILLE
GROCERY
DRINK
Coca-Cola
PRODUCE

SCOPA

109A Plaza Street
Exit Central Healdsburg east
from Highway 101, northern
side of the plaza

Tel. 707.433.5282,
scopahealdsburg.com

Serving daily 5:30 p.m.
to 10 p.m.

A VINTNER'S FAVORITE, Scopa offers beautifully simple Italian food made with the best local ingredients. Offerings range from baked goat cheese and antipasti to pizzas, home-made ravioli, and perfectly seared steaks for two ($55). Most dinner entrées are in the $15 to $20 range, lunch is a bit less, and the plaza-side ambience is charming and intimate. If you can, try to make one of their "Wine-maker Wednesdays," when an area winemaker (maybe one you've met just that morning out tasting) pitches in as guest wait-staff for the night and offers hands-on advice about delicious food-and-wine pairings.

HERE YUCATÁN-BORN chef and owner Mateo Granados serves up some excellent dishes that are a unique fusion of Latin, French, and American cooking traditions. The *San Francisco Chronicle* recently named this one of the top 100 restaurants in the entire Bay Area, so the secret is out—but who says all good things have to be a secret anyhow? There are tacos, tamales, salads, and hearty dishes with ingredients ranging from local feta and baby fennel to roasted suckling pig and stuffed squash blossoms. Most dinner plates are $15 to $25, and on warm nights try to get a seat out on the garden patio.

Maps on pages x–xi

THE RUSSIAN RIVER AVA rolls out to the west of Highway 101 along the stretch of road that runs from Santa Rosa to Healdsburg, and it takes its name from the powerful river that eventually makes its way to the sea over on the Sonoma coast. During the 1920s and 1930s, small towns along the river flourished as summer vacation resorts for the San Francisco elite, and, before that, hardy woodsmen and loggers harvested the area's redwood forests for the timber that helped build the American West.

For tourists, the Russian River—in fact, the entire region of Sonoma known to locals as "the west county"—is a magical place, where you can find ancient redwood forests, breathtaking scenery, and, of course, excellent wine tasting opportunities. This cool-climate AVA is renowned for its Chardonnay, Pinot Noir, and sparkling wines.

Although the area is crisscrossed with dozens of small roads, there are two main wine tasting circuits through the Russian River Valley. You can take either the Guerneville Road exit west from Highway 101, which will let you pick up Highway 116 in either direction, or you can follow the River Road exit west from Highway 101, which will take you along the flood plains right into the heart of the little town of Guerneville (pronounced Gurnville). From here, you can take a walk in the redwood forests that are part of the Armstrong Reserve. Or if you want to get lunch, you can follow the signs to Graton (pronounced Grayton) or, farther on, to Occidental. From Occidental, if you can't turn back without dipping your toes in the Pacific, now just ten-odd miles away, ask one of the locals how to find Coleman Valley Road. It twists and turns and winds, and then it leads you, magnificently, over a long bluff to panoramic views of the ocean.

ROBERT RUE VINEYARD

1406 Wood Road, Fulton
Exit River Road west from
Highway 101, south on Fulton
Road to the Wood Road
intersection

Tel. 707.578.1601,
robertruevineyard.com

Tasting Friday, to Sunday
10 a.m. to 5 p.m.; other days
by appointment only

THE ROBERT RUE VINEYARD is the kind of place you find by accident if you make a wrong turn somewhere. But if you follow a small residential lane, up past the old ranch houses and fields, you will know it's the right place when you see some small vineyards and a little turn-of-the-century American Gothic farmhouse with sprawling flower gardens. This is the home of Bob and Carlene Rue, who have farmed these ten acres as grape growers for thirty years. Visits take place in the barn-style tasting room just behind the home.

They bought the property as a young married couple back in the early 1970s, and Carlene will tell you with a chuckle that back then they didn't know anything about winemaking. Bob learned from the old man who sold them the land everything he needed to know about how to care for these head-pruned and historic vineyards—planted back in the last years of the nineteenth century with old field blends like Petite Sirah, Alicante Bouschet, Carignane, and mostly Zinfandel. It is one of the few vineyards of its sort to have survived the periodic phylloxera outbreaks in the county's history.

When their long-term growing contracts ended in 2000, Bob and Carlene, who run the company with their daughters and sons-in-law, decided the time had come to do more than make some family wines in the garage. Since their first release, the Robert Rue Vineyard's reserve Zinfandel (around $35)—the only wine they produce—has won dozens of medals.

The total production at Robert Rue is just a thousand cases of wine a year, and you'll often find Bob and Carlene in the tasting room. Carlene knows all the members of the wine club personally, and as you get chatting you'll soon understand why. Afterward, Bob will take you out for a tour of the vineyards, where the kids can let off some steam (but no dogs, please), and he'll tell you about the local terroir—how the evening fogs roll in from the Pacific so the grapes ripen slowly and how the hard pan in the soil makes the vines struggle just enough to produce a hearty wine with rich tannins. So bring your sturdy shoes and all your questions. This is back lane wine tasting at its most intimate and most pleasurable.

IRON HORSE VINEYARDS

9786 Ross Station Road,
Sebastopol,
Exit Guerneville Road west
from Highway 101
to Gravenstein Highway/
Rt. 116 north, west on Ross
Station Road

Tel. 707.887.1507,
ironhorsevineyards.com

Tasting daily 10 a.m. to
4:30 p.m.; estate tours
by appointment Monday to
Friday at 10 a.m.

PERCHED HIGH ABOVE the valley floor, with long views of the vineyards and oak-covered hills, Iron Horse Vineyards is a hilltop oasis, complete with swaying palm trees. Owned and operated by the Sterling family, Iron Horse makes what is easily one of the two or three best sparkling wines in all of California, and they are leading the way in the establishment of the Green Valley AVA as a premium locale for wines made in the *méthode champagneoise*. In 2007, when the *San Francisco Chronicle* ranked the "best of the west," three of their wines—two vintages of bubbly and a Green Valley Chardonnay—were among the top 100.

The loamy soil of the Green Valley and the cooler climate here in the west county produce fruit with the higher acid and delicate mineral quality that is perfect for sparkling wines. In fact, this is bubbly that can compete on the world stage. Iron Horse Vineyards made its name as a small producer in the 1980s when the Reagan White House ordered bottles of their sweeter Russian Cuvée for the summit meetings with Gorbachev. The wine, of course, was a hit, and the family still jokes that they deserve "total credit for ending the Cold War." There are also dry brut and brut rosé offerings. Best of all, as the dollar plunges, could there be a better moment for discovering excellent domestic sparkling wine? The Iron Horse bubbly starts at around $40 and their high-end tête de cuvée caps out at around $100.

While Iron Horse Vineyards is worth the visit above all for the views and the sparkling wines, they also produce a range of still wines that will give curious wine adventurers a good sense of what is unique about vintages crafted here in the Green Valley. In addition to several Chardonnay wines and Pinot Noir rosés, there are Pinot Noir standards and occasional releases of more unusual red wines, such as a small-lot Cabernet Franc or Petit Verdot. Still wines range from about $20 to upward of $100, but most are in the $30 to $50 range, and, because Iron Horse is one of the larger boutique producers, these are wines you sometimes can find back home if you discover a new favorite. The tasting fee with the tour is $20, and the tour is the way to go if you have had the chance to do some advance planning. If not, you can always sample at the outdoor tasting bar overlooking the vineyards.

MARTINELLI VINEYARDS AND WINERY

3360 River Road, Windsor
Exit River Road west from
Highway 101

Tel. 800.346.1627,
martinelliwinery.com

Tasting daily 10 a.m. to 5 p.m.

THE MARTINELLI FAMILY has been farming in the wine country since the 1860s, when Giuseppe and Luisa Martinelli came to California from their native Tuscany. By 1899, the couple had saved just enough money to buy a small tract of land on a steep hillside, where they planted their first vineyards with rootstock they had brought with them from Italy. Working the sixty-degree angle of the field was so laborious and challenging that it soon became known as Jackass Hill, and today this century-old vineyard is the steepest unterraced slope in Sonoma County—and home to some of the region's best single-vineyard-designate Zinfandel.

Most of the wines at Martinelli are, in fact, single-vineyard-designate, and today the estate winery is owned and operated by Lee Martinelli and his sons, Lee Jr. and George, now the fifth generation of family winemakers. The tasting rooms are set just off River Road in charming historic hop barns, where much of the production takes place on-site. True to their roots as growers and farmers, the family still sells 90 percent of the fruit grown on the property to other vintners. The remaining 10 percent they reserve for their own wines. In 1993 the Martinellis began an association with their neighbor and one of the county's celebrity winemakers, Helen Turley, who makes some of the finest wines in California. Today, Bryan Kvamme has taken over as winemaker, and Helen is the consulting winemaker.

The total case production at Martinelli is under twelve thousand, and the wines range from Sonoma Coast Chardonnays to classic Russian River Pinot Noir and Zinfandel wines. There are also some more unusual offerings, including a dry Gewürztraminer and a Muscat Alexandria made from the old head-pruned vines planted on Jackass Hill in the very beginning. Most wines are in the $40 to $75 range, and they are a perennial favorite with serious collectors.

DUTTON-GOLDFIELD WINERY

3100 Gravenstein Highway North, Sebastopol
Exit Highway 12 west from Highway 101, heading west on Occidental Road, north onto Highway 116 at Graton Road

Tel. 707.827.3600, duttongoldfield.com

Tasting daily 10 a.m. to 4:30 p.m.

A PARTNERSHIP BETWEEN Steve Dutton and Dan Goldfield, the Dutton-Goldfield Winery was founded in 1998 as a collaboration between one of the west county's oldest farming families and one of Sonoma County's most innovative cool-climate winemakers. Steve grew up tending the grapes on his father's Russian River vineyards. Dan studied enology at the University of California, Davis, back in the 1980s and went on to work his magic with Pinot Noir as the winemaker at La Crema. The result over the past decade has been a winery known for producing some of Russian River's most distinctive and celebrated wines, primarily excellent Chardonnay and Pinot Noir wines with smaller releases of Zinfandel and Syrah (most wines in the $30 to $75 range). *Wine and Spirits* has ranked Dutton-Goldfield as one of their 100 Top Wineries of the Year for four years running, and in 2010 *Sunset Magazine* named Dan winemaker of the year. Apart from the great wines, you'll find a friendly welcome at the low-key tasting room. Tastings range from a $15 flight (waived with purchase) to a $30 wine-and-cheese pairing option.

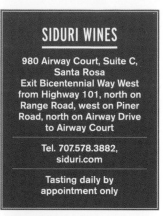

ADAM AND DIANNA LEE will tell you that they fell in love drinking wine back in their native Texas, where Adam worked in wine sales and Dianna in gourmet foods. They visited the North Bay wine country as part of that romance, and they made their first four barrels of Pinot Noir in the early 1990s from grapes they bought in the newspaper classifieds. That year Adam was twenty-eight, and Dianna was just twenty-three, but they had already immersed themselves in winemaking, scouring books for information on the technical aspects of the craft and learning firsthand by working for some of the area's other small wineries.

The story of what happened next is the stuff of legend. Adam and Dianna managed the acre of vineyards they had secured under contract, dropping most of the fruit to get intense flavors, and got lucky that year with natural fermentation and the native yeasts. The result was what they knew was a great wine—and when they heard that the celebrated wine critic, Robert Parker, was staying at a nearby hotel, they boldly dropped off a bottle for him. The result was their first great rating and the beginning of their reputation for making some of the country's best Pinot Noir.

Today, Adam and Dianna still focus on making about ten thousand cases a year of premium Pinot Noir wines, most in the $25 to $50 range, released unfiltered and unfined and made from fruit grown in vineyards as far north as Oregon and as far south as Santa Barbara. Recently, they have started up a partnership in a second winery with Dianna's family, and visitors can also sample the Novy Family Wines—mostly Syrah, Zinfandel, and Chardonnay. The emphasis in the tasting room is on good wines and not glitz, so when you visit expect to find yourself experiencing a working winery in action. Here on the production site, barrel tasting is easy. And if you become one of their direct-mail customers and can't make it back to Sonoma every spring to try the new vintage, Adam and Dianna travel regularly hand-selling their family wines and always try to arrange special wine tasting events in the cities they visit. It's the only wine club you'll find where the winemakers come to you.

PELLEGRINI FAMILY VINEYARDS

4055 West Olivet Road,
Santa Rosa
Exit River Road west from
Highway 101, south on Olivet
Road to West Olivet Road

Tel. 707.545.8680,
pelligrinisonoma.com

Winery tour and tasting
Thursday to Sunday 10 a.m. to
4:30 p.m. by appointment only

WHEN THE *San Francisco Chronicle* named the top five winemakers of 2007, Robert Pellegrini was on the list. For those who know the family and their long history as winemakers in Sonoma, it's no mystery. When Prohibition drove most small family wineries out of business in the early decades of the last century, limiting production to a mere two hundred gallons for personal use, the Pellegrinis made the most of this small loophole. If they couldn't sell wine, they could sell grapes. For decades, the family made their way as important brokers—first of grapes and, later, once again of wines.

Handsome Italian men and their smiling wives, with that fresh-scrubbed look of the 1930s and 1940s, stare out of the old family photographs that adorn the walls of the tasting room, now run by the third generation of Pellegrini winemakers.

This is a working winery, and the tasting room is in the middle of the action. It is filled with row after row of aging barrels, stacked ceiling high. The lane back to the buildings is narrow and runs through the sixty-five-acre Olivet Lane vineyards that produce the family's flagship Russian River Valley Pinot Noir ($35). Their award-winning Merlot is grown farther north, on property up in the Alexander Valley. Producing something over twenty-five thousand cases a year, they are just under the boutique threshold, and you won't be the first person to discover the Pellegrini wines. But there's a reason why they are the darlings of the critics.

RANDY PITTS GREW UP in a grape-growing family here in the Russian River Valley, where his folks have owned vineyards and ranch lands since the 1970s. His story is a familiar one in Sonoma County: a barrel of garage wine made from some grapes out back ended up selling from the vineyards. In Randy's case, the wine was Zinfandel, and that's still the focus of this small-production winery.

HARVEST MOON ESTATE AND WINERY

2192 Olivet Road, Santa Rosa
Exit River Road west
from Highway 101, south
on Olivet Road

Tel. 707.573.8711,
harvestmoonwinery.com

Tasting daily 10 a.m. to 5 p.m.

But it's the Gewürztraminer that draws most visitors to Harvest Moon Winery. Randy makes a dry Russian River Gewürztraminer and a small amount of sparkling estate Gewürztraminer, which is pretty unusual in the valley. You'll also find some small-lot Pinot Noir made from fruit grown just down the road. The wines range from $20 to $35, and if you're lucky you might arrive on one of those afternoons when Randy has the outdoor bread oven fired up. You can sample local olive oils, munch some warm bread, and taste some country-style wines far from all the rattle-and-hum.

Harvest Moon also hosts regular events from their Wine Country Classrooms (winecountryclassrooms.com), where you can register for intensive wine and olive oil tasting seminars ($20 to $80) at various locations throughout the county.

SUNCÉ WINERY

1839 Olivet Road, Santa Rosa
Exit River Road west
from Highway 101, south
on Olivet Road

Tel. 707.526.9463,
suncewinery.com

Tasting daily 10:30 a.m. to
5 p.m.

ARRIVING AT SUNCÉ, there's no missing that this is a family business. The entrance is a driveway, and the tasting room is a charming garage conversion, painted in the cheerful and welcoming hues that might serve as an emblem for the Suncé experience. In front of the house, the roses spill out of the garden. In the back and off to the sides are the vineyards: all three acres of them. The winery is a true family affair, run by the husband-and-wife team of Frane and Janae Franicevic, fourth-generation winemakers from Croatia. Those generations of experience along the shores of the Adriatic Sea show in the wines they make.

Along with the perennial Sonoma County favorites—the Cabernets, Zinfandels, and Pinot Noirs that have made the region famous—at Suncé you'll also find some unusual varietals. Their award-winning Nebbiolo ($50) is made with 100 percent of what the Italians usually think of as a blending grape. The only way to get a bottle is to visit the tasting room, and the family has had to impose a one-bottle maximum to prevent it from disappearing into cellar collections. They also make a fifty-fifty Malbec-and-Barbera blend and an award-winning Petite Sirah, both of which are worth the trip. For folks who like their white wines with just a hint of American oak, there's a nice Burgundy-style Chardonnay. And if you're looking for a good reason to open a bottle, they also release select wines under a second charity label, One World Wine for AIDS, with 25 percent of the proceeds going to nonprofit AIDS organizations (wineforaids.org).

Their small-lot single-vineyard-designate wines arc in the $20 to $50 range, and, if you call ahead for an appointment, Frane will give you the winemaker's tour or let you do some barrel tasting. Better yet, join the wine club in advance and plan your trip accordingly, because at Suncé the club members do the bottling. For your labors, you get a free case of wine, an amazing 50 percent off tasting room sales, and a once-in-a-lifetime wine country experience—unless you come back next year, too.

TARA BELLA WINERY AND VINEYARDS

3701 Viking Road, Santa Rosa
Exit River Road west from
Highway 101, south on Olivet
Road, east on Viking Road

Tel. 707.544.9049,
tarabellawinery.com

Tasting daily by
appointment only

KEVIN AND WENDY MORROW met in the wine industry here in California, at a company party back in the early 1980s, and they've been making wine together now for nearly thirty years. Up in Sonoma, they always had a favorite place in the wine country: the tiny vineyard estate owned by their friends Rich and Tara. The vineyard was down the end of a winding dirt road off a back lane, and from the house there were views of Mount St. Helena in the background. It was just the sort of place to get one dreaming. So in 2010, when their friends hinted that they were thinking about retiring, Kevin and Wendy instantly offered to buy Tara Bella and continue the tradition.

Today, the couple runs the estate, along with their youngest child, Dillon. It's a six-acre property that produces beautifully crafted wines that are unembellished and aren't heavily manipulated. Kevin adheres to the old adage that great wines are made in the vineyard, and at Tara Bella there are still just two wines, both unblended, estate-grown, vineyard-designate Cabernet Sauvignons (around $70 to $80 depending on the vintage). Reflecting the cooler climate of the region, these are bright, fruit-forward wines, with lower alcohol volumes, and in the Russian River region Cabernet Sauvignon is still a bit unusual. In competitions these wines have taken more than a dozen gold medals in recent years and have garnered a prestigious double gold. Only a few hundred cases of wine are produced each year, and they always sell out.

Tasting at Tara Bella is by appointment—but if you find yourself just around the corner and curious, it's one of those places where they welcome the last-minute phone call and will try to accommodate you if possible. Once you arrive, nothing is hurried at one of the wine country's smallest back lane wineries. You'll take a stroll through the vineyards, get to see how a wine is made, and share the experience with the people for whom this is a life passion. It's friendly, low-key, and a pretty magical way to spend an afternoon. The tasting fee is $10, applied toward any purchase.

BATTAGLINI
ESTATE WINERY

2948 Piner Road, Santa Rosa
Exit Bicentennial Way west
from Highway 101, west
on Piner Road just west of
Bacigalup Road

Tel. 707.578.4091,
battagliniwines.com

Tasting daily by
appointment only

GIUSEPPE "JOE" BATTAGLINI came to the United States in 1956 from his native Lucca, and the vineyards here—planted in 1885 by the Lagomarsino family with Zinfandel and Petite Sirah grapes—are part of Sonoma County's Italian winemaking tradition. Joe and his wife, Lucia, bought this twenty-five-acre estate in 1988 and founded a family winery in the midst of these historic vineyards. Their first vintage was in 1994, with 250 cases of wine. Today the total production is just over two thousand cases. As you might expect, this is wine crafted in the old-style Tuscan way. The grapes are dry farmed and allowed to struggle and ripen beautifully without artificial irrigation. The vines are head-pruned, and the grapes are handpicked.

It's not just that you'll find traditional Italian-style wines at the Battaglini Estate Winery. When you drive in, you feel like you are in Italy. During the barrel tasting weekend, Italian love songs blare from the small barn turned tasting room, where there are posters of Rome and Lucca on the walls, with little flags showing the streets where Joe's family still lives. If you ask about his hometown, from behind the counter he'll bring out a picture book and show you the sights, maybe even share with you his best picks for restaurants in this small town or one of his favorite recipes. He's got those laughing intelligent eyes that seem to capture the spirit of the Italians, and even on a busy day Joe and his family make sure everyone feels a part of the tasting experience. His sons pour barrel tastes out front, and it's all in good spirits. From the courtyard, you can see the shaded arbor where the family dinners must be held at the house just next to the tasting room, with the vineyards beyond.

Most years the Battaglini wine club does a trip to Lucca, led by the family, and you know it must be an amazing experience. If you can't get to Italy, here's the alternative. For the price of a week in Tuscany, you can haul home a lot of wine. Battaglini's is a piece of the old country, a place filled with conviviality and great wine. Their Zinfandels have been consistent medal winners at state harvest fairs and in national competitions, and they also produce excellent Petite Sirah, Chardonnay, and late-harvest Chardonnay wines, priced in the $20 to $50 range. You can buy futures by the case at a significant discount, and during their autumn Stomp Event fledgling winemakers can try their hands (or feet) at crushing grapes the old-fashioned way.

WOODENHEAD WINE

5700 River Road, Santa Rosa
Exit River Road west from
Highway 101, west of the
Olivet Road intersection

Tel. 707.887.2703,
woodenheadwine.com

Tasting Thursday to Monday
10:30 a.m. to 4:30 p.m.

THE EDITORS AT *Food & Wine* have fallen in love with the Woodenhead Pinot Noir wines, featuring them now for two years running in its glossy pages. And it's easy to see why. Sourcing fruit from Sonoma, Mendocino, and Humboldt counties, winemaker Nikolai Stez (a longtime veteran of the cult team at the allocation-only Williams Selyem Winery phenomenon) and partner Zina Bower specialize in premium single-vineyard-designate Pinot Noir and Zinfandel wines, as well as a French Colombard and one of the valley's best sparkling wines, made in the traditional method (in the $30 to $70 range).

The Woodenhead tasting rooms are perched up on a hillside overlooking the Russian River Valley, and you'll want to take in the views from the deck. But first, head to the bar, where the ambience is warm and rich and most days you can sample excellent handcrafted wines in surprising peace and quiet.

BACK IN THE 1950S, Joe and Annemarie Bucher established a dairy ranch here on the west side of Healdsburg, and today their son, John, and his wife, Diane, still run a farm on the property largely dedicated to milking organic cows. As you drive past the Bucher Farm, you'll also notice a whole lot of vineyards. When John came home from school after taking a degree at the University of California Davis in

BUCHER VINEYARD

5293 Westside Road, Healdsburg
Exit Central Healdsburg west from Highway 101, south on Westside Road

Tel. 707.433.4056,
buchervineyard.net

Sales by appointment only

agricultural economics and animal sciences back in the 1980s, it was clear that this area was already capable of producing world-class vineyards. So in the 1990s, the family put in their first plantings of Pinot Noir and, before long, they were selling their fruit to some of the most famous premium winemakers in the area. The wines made with grapes from the Bucher Vineyards sometimes command prices in the hundreds of dollars.

If you want to see what's so special about this terroir and the Pinot Noir that thrives here, you can now take a more direct route: the Buchers have recently started releasing just a few hundred cases a year of Pinot Noir and Chardonnay wine (around $30 to $50), mostly sold by allocation. They don't have a tasting room quite yet, but, if you want a chance to try a great wine before it becomes widely celebrated, you can call ahead to pick up a couple of bottles. Most of the better restaurants in Sonoma will let you open a special bottle for a modest corkage fee, and this is a chance to try something you won't find anywhere but in the wine country.

GRACIANNA WINERY

6914 Westside Road,
Healdsburg
Exit Central Healdsburg
west from Highway 101,
south on Westside Road

Tel. 707.486.3771,
gracianna.com

Tasting daily 11 a.m.
to 5 p.m.; Wednesday by
appointment only

TRINI AND LISA AMADOR got into the winemaking business for a reason that is a bit unusual: when their son was fifteen, they caught him in the garage making wine. They figured they had better learn what he was up to. In the way that one thing tends to lead to another in life, the family went on to found its own winery, and today at Gracianna they make about a thousand cases a year of award-winning wines. Trini is a writer as well as a winemaker (and his novel Gracianna is, they will kid you, the perfect wine pairing). The focus is on Zinfandel, Chardonnay, Sauvignon Blanc, and Pinot Noir, including an estate Pinot Noir from the premium Mercedes Riverblock Vineyard (around $30 to $50). Trini is a Sonoma County native and grew up on the Russian River, so it's no surprise that they source their fruit from this celebrated appellation. True to their origins, the tasting room is open-air and industrial—a return to the garage style where it all got started—and tucked away in a beautiful pastoral setting. The tasting fee is $10.

RUN BY THE father-and-son team of Tom and Jeremy Baker, Thomas George Estates rests on a piece of land that in the wine country is legendary. It used to be land owned by Davis Bynum, who was widely acknowledged as one of the masters of Russian River Pinot Noir and Chardonnay crafting—and as a man with an excellent eye for the terroir required to grow those varietals at a world-class level.

Today, Thomas George Estates produces Pinot Noir and Chardonnay from these vineyards, and the Baker family has expanded the estate plantings steadily, along with building eight thousand feet of new underground caves for optimal aging and storage. There are also recent releases of Sauvignon Blanc, Syrah, Viognier, Zinfandel, and Pinot Blanc on offer in the friendly tasting room. Back in the 1920s, Sonoma County was known for its beer and not its wines, and the tasting room is a converted hop mill. Old hop mills and hop kilns still dot the landscape here in the county.

Most of the wines are in the $30 to $75 range, and many of them are award winning. Although Thomas George is not one of the smallest or most rustic of the back lane wineries, this is a fabulous place to visit, especially if you didn't happen to make an appointment in advance. The location is beautifully bucolic, the welcome is warm and inviting, and you can just stop by anytime to taste the wines, enjoy the picnics tables, or take a hillside walk up the ridge. There, you can see the historic Davis Bynum vineyards and soak in the long views over the valley. Tasting is $15, waived with a purchase of $35 or more.

SANTA ROSA

Located in the heart of Sonoma County, where Highway 12 meets Highway 101, Santa Rosa is an easy drive from many of the county's most famous appellations, including the Russian River Valley and Sonoma Mountain. While not as quaint or adorable as some of the smaller towns in the area, Santa Rosa is where the locals go when they want world-class food at real-world prices. The city boasts some of the finest small restaurants in the wine country—and some of the best bargains.

ON A BUSY ROADSIDE just south of the Highway 12 junction in Santa Rosa, Dierk's Parkside Café is easy to miss. But missing it would be a mistake. Owner and chef Mark Dierkhising built his national reputation running luxury establishments in the wine country, and he now serves up the same excellent food in a casual café setting. Mark is passionate about serving unpretentious, imaginative food made with local and seasonal ingredients.

If you want a rare wine country treat, try to get a spot at one of the monthly Purveyor's Dinners. With only thirteen tables and one dinner seating, it's an intimate and unique dining experience. These evenings—featuring a four-course prix fixe menu priced at around $50 a person and showcasing the best foods of the North Bay—are so popular with the locals that you are likely to find yourself the only out-of-towner in the room. It's also a perfect occasion for anyone on a back lane wine tasting adventure: although there is a small wine and beer list, you are warmly encouraged to bring your own favorite discoveries for service tableside, and there's no corkage fee.

Mark and his wife, Karen, have also recently opened up a second location, Dierk's Midtown (1422 Fourth Street, Santa Rosa, open daily 7 a.m. to 2 p.m., dierksmidtown.com) in central Santa Rosa.

ALL THAT FANCY wine country cuisine is wonderful, but deep down we all know nothing actually goes with a fine bottle of Zinfandel as well as rustic Italian cooking. That's especially true when the pizza and antipasti happen to come from one of Sonoma County's favorite local restaurants—Rosso's Pizzeria, tucked into a shopping mall where few tourists ever wander. The restaurant is down-home, with daily specials listed on the chalkboard up front and soccer playing on the television in the afternoons, but the co-owners—Kevin Cronin and John Franchetti—come to the business with haute cuisine experience.

At the traditional lunch and dinner hours, you'll almost certainly have to wait for a seat, but one of the best things about Rosso's is the nonstop service throughout the day. If you are looking for a late lunch, this is the place to go. And in the evening, it's unquestionably worth the wait. The handmade pizzas (around $15) are made in the thin-crust Neapolitan style, with local gourmet toppings, and baked in a wood-fired oven. There is a tantalizing selection of antipasti, salads, and nightly main course specials (including, in season, oven-roasted Dungeness crab that the locals have embraced with great enthusiasm). The wine list is excellent, with many selections by the glass, and there's an emphasis on small wineries that practice sustainable viticulture. If you want to try out one of your recent tasting discoveries, the corkage is just $10. They also have a second location at Theatre Square in Petaluma (151 Petaluma Boulevard South, right in the town center).

CHLOÉ'S CAFÉ

3883 Airway Drive, Suite 145,
Santa Rosa
Exit Mendocino Avenue
north from Highway 101,
north on Cleveland Avenue
to Airway Drive, on Landmark
Executive Center

Tel. 707.528.3095,
chloesco.com

Serving Monday to Friday
8 a.m. to 5 p.m.

THE REGULARS AT Chloé's Café are definitely locals. This little bistro is set in the midst of a business park over on the west side of Santa Rosa, and there's nothing precious about the ambience. In fact, you probably wouldn't know you were in the wine country. The place feels a lot more like one of those small workingman's restaurants you find on the back roads of France. And it's no wonder. The café is owned and operated by the Pisan family, who came to Sonoma County from the south of France back in the 1960s, with generations of experience in the patisserie business behind them. Today, brothers Marc and Alain, along with Alain's wife, Renée, continue making traditional French country favorites using old family recipes.

The selection is limited—but delicious. And the focus is on great French food for real people. You can pick up delicious pastries and a boulangère sandwich with egg ($5 and under) for breakfast, and the lunch menu offers a large selection of sandwiches and salads at $10 and under, with ingredients running the gamut from duck confit to local cheeses. Each week there are some local wines available by the glass, and Marc is about as knowledgeable a connoisseur as you'll find anywhere. This is just fabulous country cooking served up with all the passion and none of the fanfare.

UNDERWOOD BAR AND BISTRO

9113 Graton Road, Graton
Exit Highway 12 west from
Highway 101, west on
Occidental Road, north to
Highway 116

Tel. 707.823.70233,
underwoodgraton.com

Serving Tuesday to Saturday
11:30 a.m. to 2:30 p.m. and
5 p.m. to 10 p.m.; late-night
menu Friday and Saturday

FOOD & WINE magazine ranked Underwood number four on the 2006 list of America's 50 Most Amazing Wine Experiences, but the gourmet gurus that year were just discovering what the locals and the area's winemakers had known for years already. In local newspaper polls, Underwood still routinely makes a sweep of the Best Restaurant, Best Cocktails, Best Bartender, and Best Wine List categories in the area.

Graton is a small and hopelessly quaint little village on the way out to the Sonoma Coast and an ideal detour if you've been wine tasting all afternoon in the Russian River Valley. The atmosphere at Underwood is country French, with an old nickel-topped bar and big mirrors where you can catch someone's eye across the room in one of those mysterious sidelong glances. The food is French-inspired as well, with everything from oysters on the half shell and a bottle of bubbly (local or imported) to farm-raised lamb and local cheeses. In summer, there is a small outdoor patio for al fresco dining, and the wine list has enough little treasures on it that you might just decide to forgo the driving and arrange your own tasting flight tableside. Dinner entrées are in the $15 to $30 range.

IF YOU'RE IN THE MOOD for a romantic dinner out amid the redwoods, you won't find anything more charming than the restaurant at the Applewood Inn. For more than a decade, their wine list has been recognized with *Wine Spectator*'s Award of Excellence, and the small back lane wineries of Sonoma County have place of pride. If you never quite made it as far as the tasting room, here is your chance to try wines made by producers such as Hanzell (page 204), Hawley (page 100), Nalle (page 20), Papapietro Perry (page 34), Pasterick (page 64), Preston (page 50), Robert Young (page 82), Selby (page 104), Siduri (page 144), Unti (page 28), Williamson (page 122), and Woodenhead (page 160).

The cuisine blends the best of California with classic French cooking. The menu also highlights seafood and beautifully done meats, along with some creative and satisfying vegetarian options. Corkage is $20 a bottle if you want to open something special you discovered along the way. Entrées à la carte are in the $30 to $40 range.

They also put together arguably the most delicious picnic basket in the wine country, but you need to order it in advance (forty-eight hours notice, $55 per person). They will include a hamper with everything you need for a picnic at one of the local wineries or quiet afternoon out at one of the nearby coastal beaches, from the lunch fixings to the corkscrew.

APPLEWOOD INN AND RESTAURANT

13555 Highway 116,
Guerneville
Exit Highway 12 west from
Highway 101, west on
Occidental Road, north
to Highway 116, south of
River Road

Tel. 707.869.9093,
dineatapplewood.com

Serving Wednesday to Sunday
5:30 p.m. to 8:30 p.m.

HANA JAPANESE RESTAURANT

101 Golf Course Drive,
Rohnert Park
Exit Golf Course Drive/Wilfred
Avenue north from Highway
101, at the Doubletree Plaza

Tel. 707.586.0270,
hanajapanese.com

Serving Monday to Saturday
11:30 a.m. to 2:30 p.m.,
Sunday to Thursday 5 p.m. to
9 p.m., Friday and Saturday
5 p.m. to 9:30 p.m.

ACCLAIMED BY THE *San Francisco Chronicle* as one of the best restaurants in Sonoma County, Hana is the place to come in the wine country if what you want is first-rate sushi done with a Californian twist. You can choose from a dazzling array of traditional sushi and sashimi rolls—or you can discover some of owner Ken Tominaga's new combinations. There is also a good selection of main course entrées that range from marinated black cod and broiled freshwater eel to rib-eye steak and pan-seared chicken. The restaurant is located just minutes from Highway 101 in the college town of Rohnert Park, in a small shopping center not far from the DoubleTree hotel. The location isn't rolling vineyards, but the décor inside is entirely classy and inviting. Sushi dinners run from around $20 to $45, and most entrées are in the $15 to $20 range.

JUST TO THE WEST AND SOUTH of Sonoma County is the neighboring county of Marin, famed for its extensive and remote beach headlands. Sometimes on the back lanes you'll find yourself before you know it on the other side of the border, and if you do, it's worth a drive down the scenic oceanside Route 1. Or plan ahead and make a day of it: Marin is famous for its oysters, and one of the best ways to get a sense of its food bounty is the culinary farm and food tour offered in West Marin. You'll visit more than half a dozen local farmers and purveyors, with private tours and tastings, and enjoy a locavore picnic on the shore. All transportation is included. Tours start at about $150, with a discount for groups of five or more people.

FIRST SET ASIDE as a natural pre-serve during the 1870s by logger and landowner Colonel James Armstrong, this state reserve is one of the last remaining vestiges of the great coastal redwood forests that once covered the Russian River Valley. It is a seven-hundred-acre old-growth grove that feels untouched by the millennia. In fact, there are trees here that have stood for many centuries, including the fourteen-hundred-year-old Colonel Armstrong tree. If you have never stood in a redwood grove and experienced the monumental silence that comes in woods this ancient and towering, it would be a pity to miss your chance now. You don't need hiking boots or heavy outdoor gear, just a warm sweater and some sensible shoes. There are plenty of easy walks through the preserve, and if you come first thing in the morning, when the fog is still creeping through the valley, you won't have to miss a minute of wine tasting either. There is a small fee for an automobile pass (under $10), with no charge for pedestrians or bicyclists.

ARMSTRONG REDWOODS STATE RESERVE

17000 Armstrong Woods Road, Guerneville
Exit River Road west from Highway 101 to Guerneville, turn north on Armstrong Woods Road

Tel. 707.869.2015, parks.ca.gov/parkindex

Open daily 8 a.m. until one hour after sunset; visitor center open daily 11 a.m. to 3 p.m.

CHAPTER 5

SONOMA VALLEY

and Los Carneros

Maps on pages xii–xiii

NESTLED BETWEEN THE MAYACAMAS range to the east and Sonoma Mountain to the west, this area was called by the indigenous people the Valley of the Moon. Today, wine lovers know it by the AVA Sonoma Valley. It was here, at the historic mission of San Francisco Solano de Sonoma in the early decades of the nineteenth century, that Spanish monks planted some of the first grapes in the wine country. In 1857 Count Agoston Haraszthy founded Buena Vista, the state's oldest winery and now a California Historic Landmark. And while today Highway 12, which runs along the valley floor from Sonoma to Santa Rosa, is one of the busiest tasting routes in the area and home to some of the most famous commercial estates in the county, don't let the big names fool you. Tucked away in corners of the valley—from storefronts on Sonoma's historic plaza to mountain vineyards far up dusty gravel roads—there are dozens of small family proprietors making wines you'll be glad you discovered.

MACLEOD FAMILY VINEYARD

P.O. Box 843, Kenwood
Vineyard tasting directions
with appointment

Tel. 707.833.4312,
macleodfamilyvineyard.com

Tasting by appointment only

BACK IN THE 1970S, when George and Greta MacLeod started out as farmers and grape growers here in Kenwood, this valley was planted to fruit trees, and the rocky soil must have seemed like an impediment to the first settlers back in the nineteenth century. But the thing about grapes is that, where the vines struggle, the fruit is all the richer for it, and that meant this ranch had great vineyard potential. For years, the MacLeod family sold their grapes to some of the famous names in the wine country. Then, in the mid-2000s, the family decided to try their hand at making their own wine from all this bounty. The results are excellent, handcrafted wines sold at some of the most modest prices you'll find in the wine country—an estate rosé, Sauvignon Blanc, Merlot, and Zinfandel (around $15 to $30). After all, not having a big mortgage has some advantages.

But the great wines are only part of the reason to visit. If I had to choose just one place in all of Sonoma County to go wine tasting, this would be my top selection. One of the family members—usually the ranch manager and mother of two, Marjorie, or the "patrone" himself, George (a spry ninety-something)— will give you a warm welcome, and tasting ($15) takes place either on the ranch house patio or up at the picnic table under the old oak tree in the vineyard. George and Greta's boys, John and Richard, and Richard's wife, Gail, are all part of the family business. You can ask anything you ever wanted to know about winemaking and grape growing, enjoy an artisanal plate of local breads, cheese, and chocolate, and sample some of the wine "grown" right here in front of you. If you make it to the ranch, plan to take your time, wear sturdy shoes if you want to feel comfortable, and tell George that I said howdy.

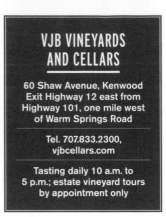

VJB VINEYARDS AND CELLARS

60 Shaw Avenue, Kenwood
Exit Highway 12 east from
Highway 101, one mile west
of Warm Springs Road

Tel. 707.833.2300,
vjbcellars.com

Tasting daily 10 a.m. to
5 p.m.; estate vineyard tours
by appointment only

WINEMAKING IN Sonoma County was once all about the Italians. These families planted what are still some of the oldest vines in the region, and they brought with them many of the traditions that characterize the North Bay crush. Then, the wine country was discovered, and today throughout the county a French winemaking style dominates. Acres of rolling vineyards are planted with Chardonnay, Pinot Noir, Cabernet, and Merlot grapes.

But if you want to try something different—and something really quite wonderful—VJB Cellars would be among those at the top of the list. The father-and-son team of Vittorio and Henry Belamonte produces less than four thousand cases of wine a year, sold only through their Tuscan-style tasting room. For the curious wine lover, VJB is a particular kind of adventure. These are wines made from varietals that are hard to find in the United States. Never had a Tocai Friulano or a Sonoma County Montepulciano? A port of Barbera? Then you have no idea what you are missing. The focus here is on old-style Italian wines in the best tradition, some crafted from vineyards more than sixty years old and most in the $25 to $50 range. And these are wines that the experts agree are special. In the past decade, they've been awarded well over a dozen gold or silver medals in international wine competitions.

At VJB the wine tasting is always about food and place, and there is a range of different options, depending on your inclination and budget. The tasting "normale" is just $10, waived with a purchase, and it doesn't require a reservation.

But if you can plan ahead, there is also an educational private tasting experience that focuses on food-and-wine pairing ($25) or even the "owner's" tasting—a chance for a private grand tour with Vittorio and Henry ($100).

KAZ WINERY

**233 Adobe Canyon Road,
Kenwood
Exit Highway 12 east from
Highway 101, north of Warm
Springs Road**

**Tel. 707.833.2536,
kazwinery.com**

**Tasting Friday to Monday
11 a.m. to 5 p.m.**

KAZ JUST MIGHT BE the hippest, happiest little winery in Sonoma County. If what you're in the mood for is good wines made by a friendly family with an exuberant sense of fun, this is just the place. It's the perfect antidote when everyone around you seems to be taking wine tasting just a little bit too seriously.

The family winery has its origins back in the 1990s. At the time, cofounder Rick "Kaz" Kasmier was a professional photographer with a serious winemaking hobby. He started out making basement wines, and in 1994 he and his wife, Sandi, decided to make a go of it. They haven't looked back. At first they poured wines out of the house, then out of some of the co-ops along Highway 12, and finally from the tasting room, which opened in 2003. Today, the business also includes their son, Ryan, who designs their funky and fun graphics.

There's nothing glitzy or pretentious here—just low-key country charm and a long, shaded terrace where you can always catch a breeze. The vineyards make up the front and back lawns. These are the original vines planted when it was still just a basement enterprise, and the family now sources fruit as well from four of their neighbors (with some grapes from Lake County thrown into the mix). They make mostly reds—Italian field varietals like Carignane, plus some Rhône-style blends using Syrah, Petite Sirah, and Petit Verdot, all in small lots. There is a Merlot, a Tempranillo, and a few varietals you've probably never tried, like Lenoir. The total production is just fifteen hundred cases a year, and they don't distribute. Most of the wines are in the $30 to $50 range, and the tasting fee is $5.

Come anytime, they will tell you. If you plan your trip at harvest, Kaz is the kind of place where visitors can get a chance to participate in the winemaking process. Try your hand at punching down some grapes on a quiet afternoon. Why not? And if you couldn't quite manage to get away without the rest of the family, kids and dogs are both welcome (juice cartons, toys, and doggie treats are kept in good stock behind the counter). Bring a picnic, pick up a bottle from the tasting room, and relax. It's all good.

MUSCARDINI CELLARS

9380 Highway 12, Kenwood
North of Warm Springs Road

Tel. 707.933.9305,
muscardinicellars.com

Tasting daily 11 a.m. to 6 p.m.

WINEMAKER AND proprietor Michael Muscardini's family has been in the Bay Area—and in the wine business—for more than a century. His grandfather, Emilio, sold wine in San Francisco after Prohibition and founded the St. Helena Napa Valley Wine Company. Today, Michael is continuing the family tradition, making just fifteen hundred cases a year of mostly classic Italian reds in the $30 to $60 range. He is one of the winemakers leading the way in the revival of Sangiovese and Barbera wines in Sonoma, and his Tuscan-style "Tesoro" (a blend of Sangiovese, Syrah, and Cabernet Sauvignon, priced at around $50) is award winning. There is also a rosé and a Pinot Grigio on offer. The estate wines come from a small one-acre vineyard up in the hills above Sonoma's Valley of the Moon, but his deep community ties and warm relationships with other local winemakers mean that Michael is able to source additional fruit from some of the best growers in the county. Conveniently located on Highway 12, right in the heart of Sonoma Valley's most famous wine tasting trail, Muscardini is an easy place to pull over and discover something handcrafted and unique. Here, meeting the winemaker doesn't just take place on special occasions. He's usually one of the guys behind the counter pouring your wine.

TY CATON GREW UP in Sonoma County and made his way back to the area in 1997, knowing exactly what he wanted to do: make wine from the grapes raised on the Caton family ranch and vineyards. Today, less than a decade after his first vintage was released, Caton farms forty acres of vineyards in the village of Agua Cali-

TY CATON VINEYARDS

8910 Highway 12, Kenwood
North of Warm Springs Road

Tel. 707.938.3224,
tycaton.com

Tasting daily 11 a.m. to 6 p.m.

ente, just ten miles south of the tasting room. The total production at Ty Caton Vineyards is just three thousand cases a year, but these small-lot wines have already earned a big reputation. His estate "Tytanium" (around $80), a blend of mainly Cabernet Sauvignon, Syrah, and Petite Sirah fruit in recent years, won both the double gold and a "Best of Class" award in the prestigious *San Francisco Chronicle* Wine Competition in 2008. His "Ty's Red" Cabernet Sauvignon (around $40) took a 2013 gold medal. In addition to a nice range of reds, Ty makes a rosé of Syrah and a Riesling (both around $30). If you can get your hands on it, the Petite Sirah dessert wine (around $40) is my favorite; it seems to beg for an old leather armchair and a roaring fire.

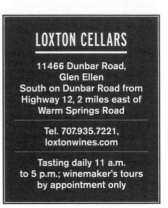

LOXTON CELLARS

11466 Dunbar Road,
Glen Ellen
South on Dunbar Road from
Highway 12, 2 miles east of
Warm Springs Road

Tel. 707.935.7221,
loxtonwines.com

Tasting daily 11 a.m.
to 5 p.m.; winemaker's tours
by appointment only

IN THE DRY summer months before the harvest, the low valleys of Sonoma turn golden, and the cars rolling down the back roads spin up clouds of dust. Heading up the small lane to the warehouse tasting room at Loxton Cellars, visitors take it slowly. And amid all the hustle and bustle of an increasingly commercialized wine country, this is a place where the pace is different.

This is the kind of place where the proprietor, Chris Loxton, a fourth-generation winemaker with Australian roots, will take you out for a walk in the vineyards and give you an education that they would charge you a couple hundred bucks for over in Napa. Wondering why the rosé is so unexpectedly dry? Come out the front doorstep, Loxton will say, let me show you those vines. Here, it is all about working with what you have and respecting the inherent qualities of the fruit and the land.

Working is the operative word at Loxton Cellars. This is not a glitzy showroom but a warehouse, winery, and sales office rolled into one (so if you want the winemaker's personal tour, be sure to call ahead so they can make time for you). The walls are lined with casks, and the tasting room used to be a garage, where the previous tenant built Formula One racecars. You are as likely as not to arrive on a day when something is going on, which is more than half the fun. The staff might be bottling the wines. Or a local restaurant owner might stop by to pick up a couple of cases. With a total production of less than three thousand cases, Loxton only distributes to local restaurants.

The focus at Loxton is on excellent handcrafted Syrah and Zinfandel wines in the $15 to $40 range, but be sure to try their port, which is exquisite. It was recently voted the best in Sonoma County. There is also a variety of food-friendly white wines and a rosé of Syrah for summer drinking.

WHEN YOU WALK IN THE DOOR at Little Vineyards, you can tell immediately that this is a special place, a winery where the music and the laughter are almost as important as the grapes. When you meet Rich Little, you understand why. He's a friendly looking man with a big smile, and he's happy to take the time to talk. And you definitely want to hear the story of this family winery and their Band Blend wine (around $20).

Rich; his wife, Joan; and her brother, Ted Coleman—the estate's winemaker—are the proprietors of Little Vineyards, which started up a few years back and makes only around two thousand cases of wine a year. Their first four hundred cases won two gold medals and a few silvers in the competitions, and it has been full steam ahead since then. Because hot artesian springs dot the property, some of that steam is literal. Rich jokes that they don't have to worry about keeping their grapes warm in the winter, and the special microclimate contributes to the hearty estate reds they produce.

The tasting room is also full of local history, and Jack London enthusiasts especially shouldn't miss out. The heart of the property is a hundred-year-old farmhouse that William Randolph Hearst built for his mother, but the bar in the tasting room comes from the old Rustic Inn in Glen Ellen, where those two legendary drinkers, Hazel Cowen and Jack London, used to tell each other whoppers. You'll also notice the musical instruments over in the corner, and if you come midweek don't be surprised if you find yourself participating in an impromptu jam session. Rich runs a recording studio out of the back of the tasting room, where luminaries like Elvin Bishop have put down tracks. Rich's band plays charity gigs locally and is a perennial favorite at the Fourth of July party on the Sonoma Plaza that the city hosts every year after the parade.

Little Vineyards focuses on making small-lot red wines, including an award-winning Syrah, a Zinfandel and Syrah blend, a Petite Sirah, and a Cabernet Sauvignon, most in the $25 to $45 range. The tasting fee is $10; try the introduction to wine tasting course with Rich if you want a real experience ($25).

If you're looking for a special place to stay in the wine country, they rent out a charming little cottage right on the property. And be sure to check out their website for Band Blend Music Nights too, when they host eats, wine, and live music in the vineyards.

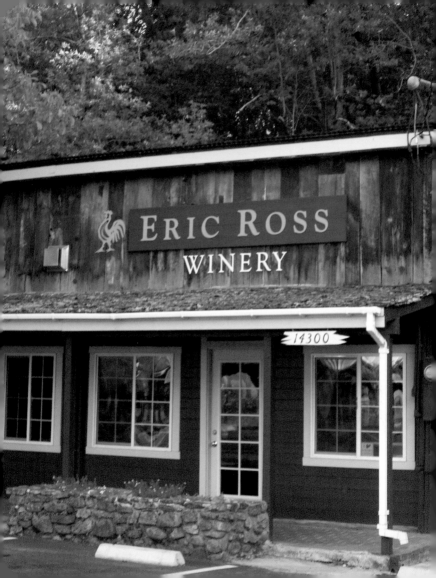

THE SUMMERS IN Northern California are hot and dry, and winemakers who don't water their vines will find themselves come harvest working with low yields—and with some of the richest and most intense fruits around. It's all part of the trade-off, and here at Eric Ross Winery, where the focus is wines made with minimal interference, some

of the unirrigated fields produce less than a ton of grapes per acre. The results are some terrific Russian River and Dry Creek wines ($25 to $50 range), including an award-winning old-vine Zinfandel, several Pinot Noir selections, and—something you won't find every day in the California wine country—a southern-French-style Marsanne and Roussane blend.

The Eric Ross tasting rooms are located just a stone's throw from Glen Ellen's Jack London State Historic Park, which has a noteworthy museum and some of the best walking trails in the county, with haunting views. The author's daughter used to live in the cottage just out behind the winery, and the tasting room still has a relaxed, home-style feel about it. You can sample at the zinc-topped bars or over on the big leather sofa, but, either way, the focus is on a friendly welcome. The winery was started out in the hills east of Occidental by two Bay Area photojournalists, Eric Luse and John Ross Storey, who used an old hand press for their first vintages. Today, the tasting room offers barrel sampling in the spring and meet-the-winemaker events throughout the year.

PETRONI VINEYARDS

990 Cavedale Road, Sonoma
Exit Highway 12 east to
Cavedale Road, just north of
Agua Caliente

Tel. 707.935.8311,
petronivineyards.com

Tasting by appointment only

AS YOU WIND all the way up rustic Cavedale Road, you'll know you've hit the home of Petroni Vineyards when you see the Italian flag waving in front of the gates. A visit to Petroni is like a little piece of Tuscany right here in California. Like so many of the Italian winemakers who came to Sonoma County in the last century, Lorenzo Petroni hails from the medieval walled city of Lucca. At the age of nineteen, he started out working in San Francisco as a busboy. Today, the restaurant he went on to build with fellow countryman, Bruno Orsi, is one of the city's most beloved landmarks: the North Beach Restaurant.

Wine Spectator has long recognized the North Beach Restaurant as having one of America's top 100 wine lists, and so it shouldn't come as any surprise that before long the Petroni family began dreaming of a vineyard in the hills of the wine country. In the early 1990s, Lorenzo knew he had found it: thirty-seven south-facing acres just across a small canyon from the legendary Monte Rosso Vineyards—a hillside estate famous since the 1880s for the superb mountain Zinfandel and Cabernet Sauvignon fruit grown in its red, iron-rich soil. For some, the old stone winery built there in 1886, on what some locals still think of as the old Goldstein Ranch, is where world-class California winemaking began. (Today, Louis M. Martini Vineyards, part of the E. J. Gallo group, owns the property, and if the view from the terrace at Petroni Vineyards isn't enough to satisfy history buffs, visits can be arranged by appointment; louismartini.com.)

Lorenzo and his wife, Maria Elena, named the new estate Poggio alla Pietra—the Hill of Rocks—and, in tribute to the family's roots and Tuscany's celebrated Brunello, Lorenzo planted the first Sangiovese Grosso clone in Sonoma. Today, the Brunelli di Sonoma ($60) is still the signature wine at Petroni Vineyards, although they also produce a small amount of Cabernet Sauvignon, Syrah, Chardonnay, Pinot Noir, and a Sangiovese-led rosé (around $15 to $80). They also make an excellent Tuscan-style olive oil ($30) made from five varieties of handpicked fruit grown on the property and cold-pressed locally in Glen Ellen. All the farming on the estate is organic, and, with even the machinery running on bio-fuel recycled from the restaurant, Petroni Vineyards is leading the way in sustainable agriculture.

But the hard work of farming isn't what comes to mind when you visit the Petroni Vineyards tasting room. Here, the cypress trees sway gently in the wind, and there are stunning views over the Sonoma Valley from the broad terraces. Some of Lorenzo's absolutely divine homemade prosciutto, fresh bread, and estate-cured olives accompany a tasting of these original and delicious vintages. Word has it that the family is soon opening a second tasting room, just off the plaza in Sonoma, if you don't make it up the mountain.

HANZELL VINEYARDS

18596 Lomita Avenue,
Sonoma
Exit Highway 12 east to
Lomita Avenue

Tel. 707.996.3860,
hanzell.com

Tasting by appointment only

CONSISTENTLY RANKED as one of Sonoma County's most prestigious wineries, Hanzell Vineyards has been at the heart of the wine revolution in California since the 1950s. Making just two wines—a Chardonnay and a Pinot Noir—they have the distinction of maintaining the longest continuous estate production in state history. Hanzell Vineyards last bought grapes in 1962, and today some of their fruit still comes from the oldest Pinot Noir vines in the New World. This is where quality winemaking in California began after Prohibition, and a visit to this two-hundred-acre hillside estate is a unique opportunity to see the past come alive.

Founded more than fifty years ago by the diplomat and industrialist James Zellerbach, Hanzell Vineyards produced its first vintage in 1957, and the intention was always to produce *grand cru* Burgundian-style wines that could compete with the best wines of Europe. In his pursuit of perfection, Zellerbach was one of the first winemakers in California to embrace some of the new technologies that went on to transform modern enology, including the introduction of French oak and stainless-steel tanks. Visitors to the winery today can still tour the historic production facility where some of the first experiments with induced malolactic fermentation began. (If you're new to that term, all you really need to know is that malolactic fermentation—known as "ML" in the industry—is the bacterial process by which apple-tart malic acid in a wine is transformed into buttery lactic acid. If you like a buttery Chardonnay, ML is one part of how it happens.)

Today, the proprietor at Hanzell Vineyards is Alexander de Byre, and the estate produces around six thousand cases a year of what is broadly recognized as some of the most cellar-worthy wines in Sonoma County (typically in the $45 to $100 range). *Wine Enthusiast* rated their 2006 Chardonnay a whopping 96 points, and the *San Francisco Chronicle* named the 2010 one of the top 100 wines of the vintage. Occasional special releases are available only to collectors and club members, often with a case minimum.

Visits are by private appointments and start at around $45, which includes a personalized tasting and a guided tour of a heritage estate that helped create the Californian wine country. There is also a two-and-a-half-hour premium-tier tasting ($150) that is a rare chance to taste some of their reserve and library wines and to do a barrel tasting. Reservations are recommended at least a month in advance. If you're looking for a luxury experience and a chance to be part of Californian winemaking history, this is the place for serious aficionados and would-be collectors.

LOS CARNEROS

With one foot in Sonoma County and the other foot in Napa, Los Carneros—the rams, in Spanish—is cooled on hot summer days by the fog that rolls in from San Pablo Bay. The result is a cool-climate terroir at the very southern tip of the wine country, an area famous for its Pinot Noir, Chardonnay, and sparkling wines. Just minutes from historic Sonoma Plaza, Highway 121/12 runs east to west across the appellation and is home to some of the North Bay's most exciting and easily accessible small wineries.

NICHOLSON RANCH WINERY

4200 Napa Road, Sonoma
Exit Highway 12 north to
Napa Road

Tel. 707.938.8822,
nicholsonranch.com

Tasting daily 10 a.m. to 6 p.m.

RISING UP ABOVE Highway 12 just where the Sonoma Valley appellation meets Los Carneros, the stucco visitors' center at Nicholson Ranch Winery gives the impression of a large commercial operation. And the estate is undeniably impressive. This is not homespun charm but pure wine country elegance. The tasting rooms are set in the midst of thirty acres of estate vineyards, with spacious windows that look out onto a lake and then beyond to the oak-covered slopes that rise above the valley. In the far distance you can just catch sight of the family's private hillside chapel, built in the Greek style by Socrates Nicholson (hiking tours just once a year; ask to be added to the list if you're keen). Today, his daughter, Ramona Nicholson, with her husband, Deepak Gulrajani, are the owners and proprietors of the family estate.

Even though the winery is state-of-the-art and luxurious, the winemaking here is still an intimate and personal affair. The Nicholson family produces less than eight thousand cases a year, and all the wines are made on-site, using a five-level gravity-flow system that was designed to bring out the delicate complexity of their signature Pinot Noir wines. In addition to estate and

Sonoma Pinots (around $40 to $50), they pour a delicious Chardonnay (also around $50) that is the perfect drink for a long summer afternoon.

Don't rush the tasting experience. At Nicholson Ranch, the emphasis is on wine education and savoring your visit. There are several different tasting options. The $10 vintner's tasting includes a flight of four wines. If you manage to plan ahead and make a reservation, there are also sit-down private tastings, some down by the lake, others including a romp through the vineyards, and for larger parties they'll even host you for lunch with enough notice (most premium tasting experiences are $15 to $40, except the lunches, which depend on your palate). Afterward, you can stroll upstairs to the art gallery that features a rotating display of contemporary Californian artists, or make a reservation for a tour of the underground caves, which are built forty-five feet into the soil and provide the perfect storage conditions for fine wines in the making.

ROBLEDO FAMILY WINERY

21901 Bonness Road,
Sonoma
Exit Highway 116 west to
Bonness Road, just north of
the Highway 121 intersection

Tel. 707.939.6903,
robledofamilywinery.com

Tasting Monday to Saturday
10 a.m. to 5 p.m. and
Sunday 11 a.m. to 4 p.m.
by appointment only

FOUNDED BY Reynaldo and Maria Robledo—and run today with the help of their nine children—the Robledo Family Winery really is just that: a family winery. From one end of the county to the other, winemakers will tell you that their story is at the heart of what makes Sonoma special. On the back lanes, hard work and talent still count for more than deep pockets and venture capital backing. At the Robledo Family Winery, that hard work and talent started when sixteen-year-old Reynaldo came to California from his home state of Michaocán to work in the vineyards. Picking grapes paid just over a dollar an hour, and he worked seven days a week to help support his family in Mexico, working his way up to vineyard foreman. After thirty years in the industry, he bought his first thirteen acres of land in Napa's Carneros region in 1984, and today the Robledo family makes six thousand cases a year of estate wine, from grapes grown on two hundred acres of land in Napa and Sonoma counties.

As the first winery in the United States owned by a migrant working family—and as one of the few Latino-owned estates in California's wine country—the Robledo Family Winery is a source of particular local pride in this part of the valley. When the tasting rooms opened in 2003, the mayor of Napa declared the occasion Robledo Family Winery Day. Even the president of Mexico, Felipe Calderon, put the tasting room on the itinerary during his visit to Sonoma County.

Those tasting rooms celebrate the family's Mexican heritage. Visitors gather around a long wooden table, and at this family-run business the emphasis is on a warm and intimate wine experience. You can come for the traditional tasting, of course. But on quiet days, they are happy to take you out for a vineyard tour ($45, reservations required), and you'll get a chance to taste their wines, too. There are also special educational food-and-wine tasting opportunities ($40). Their estate Sauvignon Blanc (just over $20) is a gold medal winner; the Carneros Pinot Noir is also lauded consistently for its quality. But there are lots of offerings—ranging from a Tempranillo and a sparkling wine to a range of dessert wines. Most wines are in the $20 to $45 range, though some of the special bottles go as high as $150. They also source some grapes from Lake County, and that lets the family offer some varietals you might not have had a chance to sample on your back lane adventures. At nearly 30 percent off retail, their wine club also has one of the most generous discounts in the county.

HOMEWOOD WINERY

23120 Burndale Road,
Sonoma
Highway 12 east to
Burndale Road

Tel. 707.996.6353,
homewoodwinery.com

Tasting daily 10 a.m. to 4 p.m.

THE HOUSE PHILOSOPHY at Homewood Winery is "the redda the bedda," and this small winery is more or less a one-man show. The heart of the enterprise is Dave Homewood, who started out making garage wines back in the early 1980s, and more than thirty years later things at Homewood Winery are still low-key and hands-on. The total production is just around three thousand cases a year, and this is very much a word-of-mouth kind of place, loved by the locals and by weekend visitors from San Francisco. These days, Dave makes about a dozen different wines, ranging from a Carneros Pinot Gris to a late-harvest Lake County Albarino. The reds run the gamut from Carneros Syrah and Dry Creek Zinfandel to a Merlot port, all in the $20 to $45 range.

Above all, Homewood eschews all things commercial. The wines are sold only from the tasting room, and it's a point of pride here that there's no advertising budget. Dogs and children are welcome. Tasting is $5, applied toward your purchase, and you'll get to sample six different wines. These are wines that are meant to go with good home cooking, and, if you want to pick up a case, there's just a simple 20 percent discount. No need to join a wine club. And those cardboard wine shippers that you might need to get all your discoveries back home? Dave sells them at cost. It's the best deal in the wine country.

AUTEUR WINES

373 First Street West, Sonoma
Exit Highway 121 north to
Highway 12, just off northwest
corner of the plaza

Tel. 707.938.9211,
auteurwines.com

Tasting daily 10 a.m. to 4 p.m.
by appointment only

FOR YEARS, Kenneth Juhasz built his reputation as an acclaimed vintner throughout Sonoma County, where his wines earned one accolade after another. He is still the consulting wine-maker for some special projects—including Donum Estate and Dustan (page 220). But about a decade ago he and his wife, Laura, established their own label, and in just a decade Auteur Wines has garnered a reputation for making premium Pinot Noir and Chardonnay (from about $30 to $75). They make fewer than two thousand cases a year, mostly from fruit sourced in coastal Sonoma and Mendocino appellations, and until recently their tasting room was a secret hideout for wine devotees. Now their 1915 winery cottage is open for limited tastings by appointment (email laura@auteur-wines.com), and it's a sit-down-meet-the-winemaker-type affair (around $25), where you get a chance to try some of their recent releases and learn more about what makes Sonoma County a special winegrowing region.

IN THE 1990S IN BORDEAUX, the hip term for the small, craft-focused vintners leading innovation was the "garagistes" because they made their wines in their garages. Today throughout Sonoma County, you'll find some of the best wines around being made in small warehouse spaces. No one has invented a fancy word for it yet, but the critics were quick to recognize the great quality coming out of some of these warehouses. The wines made by Katy Wilson of La Rue Wines—crafted in a working winery space just south of Sonoma Plaza and sourced from grapes on the Sonoma Coast—have been especially lauded in recent years.

LA RUE WINES

21692 Eighth Street East, Suite 300, Sonoma
Heading east on Highway 12, north on Eighth Street East

Tel. 707.933.8355, laruewines.com

Tasting by appointment only

Katy knew she wanted to be a winemaker by the time she was eighteen and, after studying enology, quickly went on to work for some of the big names in the world of winemaking. She is still the associate winemaker at the award-winning Kamen estate. Just recently, though, Katy started making one wine of her own: a highly rated Pinot Noir (from $60 to $70, varying by vintage), made from fruit grown just a few miles from the Pacific. In this unique climate, the Pinot Noir is special. The fruit is intense, but there is something just a bit more austere and mineralic about it. She's looking to start making a Chardonnay soon.

After a behind-the-scenes glimpse at a working winery, tasting is a down-to-earth experience in the conference room, where you'll get a chance to ask Katy to tell you more about her story and about the wines that she's making. Tasting is $15, waived with the purchase of two or more bottles.

DUNSTAN WINE / DURELL VINEYARD

P.O. Box 1676, Sonoma
Directions provided with appointment

Tel. 707.933.3839,
dunstanwines.com

Tasting by appointment only

BACK AT THE BEGINNING of the twentieth century, when the cheerful ranch house that is home to Dunstan Wine was built, there was no such thing as an AVA. There was just good land—in one direction Sonoma Mountain, in the other the coast and valley. But good land in the wine country is just about everything, and it turned out that these four hundred acres would before long become legendary as the Durell Vineyard. It's widely acknowledged to be some of the most exciting and important terroir in Sonoma County. Today, it uniquely straddles three of the county's appellations, the Sonoma Coast, Sonoma Valley, and Los Carneros regions.

The Durell Vineyard has a long and celebrated history, and its grapes make their way into several different well-known wine projects, but the Chardonnay and Pinot Noir fruit from the aptly named Ranch House Block—planted around the original ranch house on the property—is what makes Dunstan wines so special. Run by Ellie Price and her husband, Chris Towt, Dunstan produces fewer than a thousand cases of wine each year, and their focus is naturally on the Chardonnay and Pinot Noir grapes that grow just outside their doorstep. These are wines that have already garnered serious accolades and a passionate following—as well as points regularly in the 90s. The Chardonnay ($40) is brightly mineralic and structured to age beautifully; the Pinot Noir ($50) has the earthy notes that express so well in the Carneros. There is also a summer rosé ($25) perfect for drinking on the ranch porch and watching the sunset.

Dunstan is named after St. Dunstan—the saint who made a deal with the devil that horseshoes over a doorway would protect the inhabitants—and for Ellie there's another reason that was the perfect symbol: she's a nationally known figure in the movement to protect wild horses on public lands in the West.

Tasting at Dustan is by appointment only. The price depends on your interests, and, if you want to see a bit of a Sonoma County legend on the back lanes, it's a perfect way to spend an afternoon in the wine country.

HAWKES WINERY

**383 First Street West
Sonoma Plaza
Exit Highway 12 north from
Highway 121, west on West
Napa Street, north on First
Street West at Sonoma Plaza**

Tel. 707.938.7620,
hawkeswine.com

Tasting daily 11 a.m. to 6 p.m.

IF YOU DIDN'T MAKE IT OVER to the Alexander Valley tasting room of the Hawkes family (page 80), you have a second chance to sample their wines here on Sonoma Plaza, where in recent years more and more vintners have been setting up chic tasting salons. The Hawkes tasting room is on the northwest corner of the plaza.

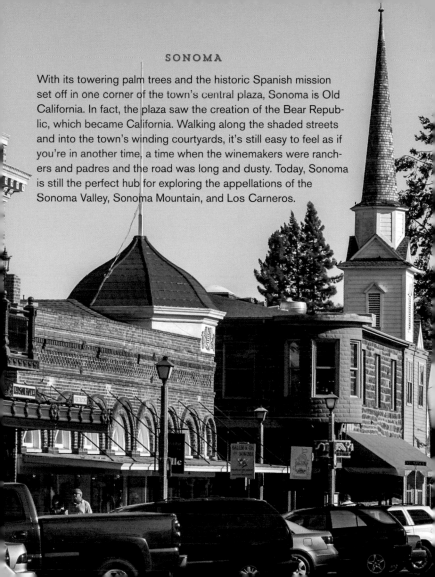

SONOMA

With its towering palm trees and the historic Spanish mission set off in one corner of the town's central plaza, Sonoma is Old California. In fact, the plaza saw the creation of the Bear Republic, which became California. Walking along the shaded streets and into the town's winding courtyards, it's still easy to feel as if you're in another time, a time when the winemakers were ranchers and padres and the road was long and dusty. Today, Sonoma is still the perfect hub for exploring the appellations of the Sonoma Valley, Sonoma Mountain, and Los Carneros.

LA SALETTE

452 First Street East, Suite H
Exit Highway 12 north from
Highway 121, east on East
Napa Street, north on First
Street East at Sonoma Plaza

Tel. 707.938.1927,
lasalette-restaurant.com

Serving lunch and dinner
daily; times vary seasonally

TUCKED AWAY IN a little courtyard off the east side of the Sonoma Plaza, visitors in search of something just a bit unique in the wine country will find La Salette and chef Manuel Azevedo's innovative Portuguese cuisine. Here, you have your choice of patio dining on a warm summer's evening or a cozy table by the wood-fired oven, and the emphasis is on local seafood with a transatlantic twist. The signature dish is a white bean and seafood stew, served in a traditional copper bowl, and of course they offer hearty helpings of *caldo verde* for lighter appetites. The cheese and charcuterie plates are also a tasty treat, and what would anywhere in Sonoma be without a great wine list? It's a blend of local favorites and some new Portuguese discoveries, including red and white tasting flights and a large selection of after-dinner Madeira, port, and Muscatel wines if you're not quite done sampling for the day. Most entrées are $25 or under.

WITH JUST OVER thirty seats in the dining room and a stellar reputation, Café La Haye is the bustling and intimate kind of place where reservations are a must. And in recent years, this local bistro has started getting the sort of big reviews that explain the posh crowd. When you taste the food, you'll understand why the *New York Times* is raving about this little café just off Sonoma Plaza.

The cooking is California-inspired Italian, with an emphasis on fresh seafood, including a house-smoked trout starter and a daily fish entrée. You can also savor traditional Tuscan pastas, local quail, or a signature hangar steak. The entrées are in the $20 to $25 range, and the wine list features many of the county's most prestigious small producers, along with an extensive (and expensive) list of reserve wines. Several of my favorite back lane wineries are sold on the list by the bottle, and it's also a super chance to try wines by the glass from some of the county's smallest vintners. If you're there on a summer afternoon, be sure to try the Grenache made by Mathis (mathiswine.com). Peter Mathis doesn't have a tasting room and doesn't distribute his wines, but he's been crafting great small lots that have been a local favorite for years. Or ask the sommelier to point you to some other undiscovered finds from the wine country.

THE FREMONT DINER

2698 Fremont Drive, Sonoma
At Carneros Highway/
Highway 121 west of the
Ramal Road intersection

Tel. 707.938.7370,
thefremontdiner.com

Serving Monday to
Wednesday 8 a.m. to 3 p.m.,
Thursday to Sunday 8 a.m.
to 9 p.m.

IN THE SHORT while that it's been open, the Fremont Diner has become a local landmark, and don't let its unassuming character fool you. This is a low-key foodie's paradise, with a bit of old-school Americana nostalgia. There's breakfast and lunch, and from 3 p.m. to 6 p.m. Thursday to Sunday one of the county's best happy hours. Breakfast standards run about $5 to $15, and at lunch it's Nashville chicken and fried catfish or (who can resist the pun) a signature Knuckle Sandwich (beef knuckle, arugula, horseradish, and ginger pickle beets), mostly in the $10 to $15 range. Beers are under $5, and of course there's local wine. After all, this is Sonoma.

RUN BY CHEF Ari Weiswasser and his wife, Erinn Benziger-Weiswasser, the Glen Ellen Star is tucked away in the small and charming village of Glen Ellen, but this is the kind of place locals from the other side of the valley will drive over to eat at. If you find yourself in the area, take the detour. There are wood-oven-roasted dishes, ranging from fish and meats to vegetables (most entrées $20 to $25), and it's all just fresh and local and lovely.

GLEN ELLEN STAR

**13648 Arnold Drive
Downtown Glen Ellen
Highway 121 to Arnold Drive,
north of Warm Springs Road**

Tel. 707.343.1384,
glenellenstar.com

**Serving dinner Sunday to
Thursday 5:30 p.m. to 9 p.m.,
Friday and Saturday 5:30 p.m.
to 9:30 p.m.**

THE ART AND NATURE preserve established by Rene and Veronica di Rosa opened to the public in 1997, and today it houses an important collection of contemporary art, with an emphasis on Northern California artists. Like so much in the wine country, the estate—which includes more than two hundred acres of wildlife preserve—started out as a vineyard. When the di Rosa family bought the property back in the 1960s, it still included the old winery that once served as the crush pad for hundreds of acres of vines planted before Prohibition. They replanted grapes, renovated the nineteenth-century buildings, and set about growing fruit and collecting art. Eventually, as the collection grew, the vineyards were sold to one of the big commercial outfits in Napa, and the bulk of the estate opened to the public as part of a preservation trust. Today, there are several thousand works of art on display and an active program of gallery tours, special exhibits, and nature hikes to the summit of Milliken Peak, where you can enjoy dazzling views of the Napa River and San Pablo Bay amid the springtime wildflowers and summer grasses.

THE DI ROSA PRESERVE

5200 Sonoma Highway, Napa
Exit Highway 12 east from
Highway 101, just east of
Calistoga Road

Tel. 707.226.5991,
dirosaart.org

Open Wednesday to Sunday
10 a.m. to 6 p.m., closes at
4 p.m. April to October
Admission $10 to $15

Wine Shipping Services

ALL WAYS COOL

3350 Coffey Lane, Suite B, Santa Rosa
Tel. 707.545.7450 • allwayscool.com

There are lots of ways to get your back lane wine purchases home, but one of the simplest is a third-party wine shipping service. Any premium winery can recommend someone to you, and, if you are planning to buy and send home several cases of wine, working with a consolidator can make the whole experience a lot more fun and less expensive. My personal favorite is All Ways Cool in Santa Rosa, which has very smart staff that can also help you down the road when you might want to reorder some of your back lane favorites.

The way it works at All Ways Cool is that you go out tasting and choose the wines you want. Then, you can either collect the bottles in your hotel room, or you can leave your case purchases right at the winery for pickup later. At the end of your trip, you just need to tell All Ways Cool where you've left the wines and where you need them sent. Someone on the staff will go and get them for you from pretty much anywhere in Sonoma County, including your hotel or B&B. Because you can send all the wines from your tasting trip in one single shipment, it is generally more cost-effective than having individual cases mailed from the wineries, and they can often arrange delivery to states that don't allow direct shipments from the tasting room.

During the hot summer months, shipping wines to certain parts of the country is a dicey business, and, for a small monthly charge per case, All Ways Cool will also keep your cases in climate-controlled storage until the cool weather comes. If you are buying futures that need to get fetched from the wineries and mailed in the autumn (and some wineries want you to pick up futures on a particular weekend), this can be an elegant solution. Shipping rates depend on actual weight and location, and as a general rule folks will tell you that it is much less expensive to ship to a business address. The costs are based on standard commercial shipping rates, plus a modest handling fee. If you are going to do some serious wine tasting and stock up those cellars, this is the way to go.

UPS

ups.com/wine

It might not be elegant, but UPS has also provided consistently great service from any of the small UPS stores scattered across the wine country, from Rohnert Park and Petaluma to Santa Rosa. You can find a location and details online (ups.com/wine) or look for the sign that says "Wine Shipping" that most of them display. They will pack the wines for you and ship them directly back home at their regular commercial rates. It's almost always a better deal if a winery ships a case for you directly, but if you find you need to do the shipment yourself, either due to state regulations or smaller purchase quantities, then UPS is a great option.

LALA WINES

lalawines.com

Over a dinner in Paris, a French friend once bemoaned the impossibility of traveling with more than a bottle or two of Californian fine wine, and many visitors to the wine country are from outside the United States. Out of compassion for our European friends (and there are many who come to the wine country and find themselves stymied by all the customs-related complications of getting wines back home), some friends in New York City founded Lala Wines, an export company that specializes in delivering cases of those yummy small-lot California Cabernets (and any other varietal you fancy) back to the European Union at an affordable price via climate-controlled sea shipments and with customs clearances. As one of the founders, I'm not precisely objective, but Lala Wines has a lot of fans among the world's more far-flung wine lovers.

About the Author & Photographer

TILAR MAZZEO is the Clara C. Piper Associate Professor of English at Colby College and the bestselling author of books on wine, luxury, and French history, including *The Widow Clicquot, The Secret of Chanel No. 5, The Back Lane Wineries of Napa, The Hotel on the Place Vendôme,* and the forthcoming *Irena's Children.* She divides her time between California wine country, Maine, and British Columbia.

PAUL HAWLEY is a wine-country native, raised on his family's vineyard in Sonoma's Dry Creek Valley. He graduated from the University of California, Santa Cruz, in 2003 with a degree in film production. His feature film, *Corked,* debuted in 2008. Most days he can be found behind his lens or at his family's Hawley winery.

Index

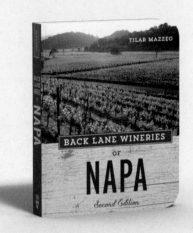